Addiction Recovery Journal

Ancient Wisdom and Today's Jokes
For Happy, Joyous and Free Folks

Materials Written, Compiled & Edited

James Bars

Home of Love Publications

Copyrights, Permissions, Disclaimer and Warning:

Many of the jokes in this journal book were adapted from jokes I have heard on AA, NA and Al-Anon speaker tapes, and also from attendance at AA, NA and Al-Anon Meetings, and from the AA *Grapevine* magazine.

ISBN: 978-0-9817534-8-5

Cover Picture: Fotilia
Interior Design: Blake Bars and Nathaniel Tainter
Cover Design: Nathaniel Tainter
Interior Illustrations: Alison Fowler

Published by Home of Love Publications
Cove, Oregon 2015

MyNewMADFATs.com

A Special Message to All Readers:

Those of you in recovery from addiction know that the solution is a spiritual one.

Dr. Bob and Bill W. were the cofounders of the most successful program of recovery to find its way into the modern world. However the means that they used were from the ancient world. They discovered through Scripture *the Power* that would lead them out of their personal hell. This Power is the same one that has existed forever. Here is a quote from the book **Pass It On,** the story of Bill Wilson and how the A.A. message reached the world (p. 147).

"Bill now joined Bob and Anne in the Oxford Group practice of morning guidance sessions together, with Anne reading from the Bible. *"Reading ... from her chair in the corner, she would softly conclude, 'Faith without works is dead.'"* As Dr. Bob described it, they were convinced that the answer to our problem was in the Good Book. To some of us older ones, the parts that we found absolutely essential were the Sermon on the Mount, the 13th chapter of First Corinthians, and the Book of James." The Book of James was considered so important, in fact, that some early members even suggested "The James Club" as a name for the Fellowship."

This humble journal book includes many pieces of information that are quoted from the Ancient Wisdom found in The Holy Scriptures. Please don't allow any pre-conceived ideas you may have, block you from the Sunlight of the Spirit. Instead, absorb the information here with an honest heart, an open mind, and a willing spirit. The goal here is to not only create a fun way to journal, but also to share with you the peace and security that comes by knowing the Lord and finding a deeper understanding of his will for you and the power to carry it out.

When Bill Wilson and the 100 other early members of Alcoholics Anonymous wrote the Big Book, they knew this Ancient Wisdom. On page 63 of that book they write, *"As we felt new power flow in, as we enjoyed peace of mind, as we discovered we could face life successfully, as we became conscious of His presence, we began to lose our fear of today, tomorrow or the hereafter. We were reborn. We were now at step three."*

This statement appears immediately before the third step prayer. I believe that Bill was talking about losing his fear of the hereafter because he had found not only *the Power* he needed to overcome his addiction to alcohol, but also the love he sought to fill his heart and the Way of that guaranteed his life would continue beyond this earth.

I do not desire to share with you my religion. I wouldn't walk across the room to share my religion with you. However, I would walk a long way to share my Lord with you.

On page 191 of the third edition of the Big Book in the story entitled Anonymous Number Three, this statement is made by the first person that Bill and Dr. Bob carried the message to. *"Bill looked across at my wife, and said to her, "Henrietta, the Lord has been so wonderful to me, curing me of this terrible disease, that I just want to keep talking about it and telling people."*

Bill was very, very grateful that he had been released from this terrible thing. He gave the Lord all the credit for having done it. He was so grateful, he wanted to tell other people about it.

Bill's statement, *"The Lord has been so wonderful to me, curing me of this terrible disease, that I just want to keep talking about it and telling people,"* has been a sort of a golden text for the A.A. program and for me." On page 20 of the same book, Bill writes, *"Our very lives, as ex-problem drinkers, depend upon our constant thought of others and how we may help meet their needs."*

These two statements reside at the heart of this humble work. The Lord has been so wonderful to me, curing me of this terrible disease, that I just want to keep telling people about Him.

Reborn,
James Bars

Dedication

I would like to dedicate this book to my Best Friend—God. Without His patient love and unshakable pursuit of me, I would have no hope. My life's goal is to hug Him one day and whisper in His ear, "Thank You."

To my beautiful, happy wife, Suzanne. "Thank you for teaching me how to love and trust again. I will love you forever." "Swuddie"

To my six children, Dana, Carly, Blake, Ashleigh, Sadie and Sissy. "I look forward to spending eternity with each and all of you. I love you. Dad."

To my sponsor "Jerry" M. who taught me how to live like a human being and showed me the ways to survive the ravages of sobriety.

To my Father and Mother and my brothers and sisters: Danny, Peggy, Terry, Sam, Bill and Don. "Thank you for teaching me how to make the best of a sometimes difficult situation."

To Ralph H. of Lewiston. We started our drinking careers together. Ralph, I pray that you are granted the precious gift of sobriety.

Home of Love Publications

MyNewMADFATs.com

A suggested way to use this book.

Read a page each day and allow your mind to ponder the thoughts expressed there and how they may apply to you and your desire to grow in your spiritual journey. Then begin to journal as your mind reflects on the thoughts for the day.

The Kingdom of God is within you.
Have fun as you open the doors of your soul to Him.

"It is through the pen that we discover the Light."
—Linda T.

May God bless and encourage you on your way home.
James Bars

Journal

Date _____

Chuckle A cop pulls over a drunk driver whom he has stopped repeatedly and says, "Show me your license, Jim Bob."

"Will you guys get your act together?" slurs Jim Bob. "Yesterday you take it away, and today you want me to show it to you!"

Wisdom _"His divine power has given us everything we need for life and godliness through our knowledge of him who called us by his own glory and goodness. Through these he has given us his very great and precious promises, so that through them you may participate in the divine nature and escape the corruption in the world caused by evil desires."_

— 2 Peter 1:3-4 (NIV)

This is me ...
When I stay on God's path, I never fall.

Journal

Date _____

Chuckle If I could drink like a normal person, I'd drink all the time.

Wisdom _"Yesterday is history, tomorrow is a mystery, today is a gift of God, which is why we call it the present."_
—Bill Keane

This is me ...
I strive to do the next right thing.

Journal

Date _____

Chuckle Letting Go: Giving up all hope for a better past.

Wisdom *"When pride comes, then comes disgrace, but with humility comes wisdom."*

— *Proverbs 11:2 (NIV)*

This is me ...
I keep no record of wrongs.

Journal

Date _____

Chuckle During his first day in a treatment facility, in the country, a shaky drunk sat fishing in a flower bed.

A visitor walking by asked, "How many have you caught?"

Answered the fisherman, "You're the fourth."

Wisdom *"A man who lacks judgment derides his neighbor, but a man of understanding holds his tongue."*
— *Proverbs 11:12 (NIV)*

This is me ...
I speak only positive words to everyone I meet. My internal dialogue is always inspiring and uplifting.

Journal

Date _____

Chuckle It was twilight in the desert. Jim Bob leaned over and gazed passionately into the sweet eyes of his date.

"Getting high," he said, "makes you look beautiful."

"I'm not high," she said.

"I know, "said Jim Bob, "but I am."

Wisdom *"We are what we repeatedly do. Excellence, then, is not an act, but a habit."*

— *Aristotle*

This is me ...
I seek to develop beneficial habits.

Journal

Date _____

Chuckle My sponsor could be a lot like Socrates: He was a very wise. He spent most of his time sharing his wisdom by giving people advice. He was poisoned.

Wisdom *"A generous man will prosper; he who refreshes others will himself be refreshed."*

— *Proverbs 11:25 (NIV)*

This is me ...
I give to others, knowing that whatever I give, will come back to me better than when I gave it.

Journal

Chuckle Two girl friends were out drinking on "girls night out" when one suddenly tumbled off her bar stool and landed unconscious on the floor.

"One thing about my friend," the other drunk slurred to the bartender, "Nobody can say she doesn't know when to quit!

Wisdom *"The journey of a thousand miles begins with a single step."*

— Lao Tzu

This is me ...
People find me enjoyable and fun to be around.

Journal

Date _____

Chuckle My Al-Anon sponsor has always told me that "the only way that I can coast, is downhill."

Wisdom _"One man gives freely, yet gains even more; another withholds unduly, but comes to poverty."_
— _Proverbs 11:24 (NIV)_

This is me ...
I give and then I get back—it never fails.
— _Proverbs 11:24 (NIV)_

Journal

Date _____

Chuckle Jim Bob went to a monastery to find a safe place to stop drinking, but he was only allowed to speak two words per year. At the end of the first year he told the elders, "Cold floors." At the end of the second year he said, "Bad food." At the end of the third year he went to the elders and declared, "I quit."

"Good," they said, "you have done nothing but complain since you arrived."

Wisdom _"All the beautiful sentiments in the world weigh less than a single lovely act."_

— James Russell Lowell

This is me ...
Every day I realize the true joy of the Golden Rule: Do to others what I would like them to do to me.

Journal

Date _____

Chuckle Alcohol Warning Label:
"Warning: The consumption of alcohol may make you think you can converse without spitting."

Wisdom *"The Lord detests lying lips, but he delights in men who are truthful."*

— *Proverbs 12:22 (NIV)*

This is me ...
Only beautiful and uplifting truth comes from my heart and mouth.

Journal

Date _____

Chuckle Why did the turkey cross the road? To prove he wasn't chicken.

Why did the turkey go to Alcoholics Anonymous? To get to the other side.

Wisdom *"People can alter their lives by altering their attitudes."*

— *William James*

This is me ...
The useful and the beautiful are never separated. I am useful.

Journal

Date _____

Chuckle Drunken Jim opened a 24-hour liquor store. Bob came staggering up to the door one morning about three a.m. as Jim was closing up. Bob said, "Hey, the sign says that you are open 24 hours!"
"Yeah," says Jim, "but not in a row."

Wisdom *"If one advances confidently in the direction of his dreams, and endeavors to live the life which he has imagined, he will meet with a success unexpected in common hours."*
— *Henry David Thoreau*

This is me ...
I know that whatever I set my mind to, and take action on, will become a reality.

Journal

Date _____

Chuckle A drunken grandmother was kicking back on the beach having a drink or two or three and watching her grandchild playing in the water.

Suddenly, a large wave came and washed the child out to sea. The grandmother slurred out to God, "Please save my precious grandchild!"

Just as suddenly, the grandchild was washed back up on the shore, safe and sound.

The drunken grandma raised her eyes toward heaven and said, "He had a hat."

Wisdom _"Diligent hands will rule, but laziness ends in slave labor."_

— _Proverbs 12:24 (NIV)_

This is me ...
I not only work hard, I also work smart by having a list of the most important things to do each day and then doing them.

Journal

Date _____

Chuckle Q: How many drug addicts does it take to change a light bulb? A: Just one—she puts it in the socket and waits for the world to revolve around her.

Wisdom *"Blessed is the man who finds wisdom, the man who gains understanding, for she is more profitable than silver and yields better returns than gold."*

— *Proverbs 3:13-14 (NIV)*

This is me ...
I treat everyone I meet as if they were one of the most important people in the world.

Journal

Date _____

Chuckle Three world views:
The pessimist's:
The cup is half empty.
The optimist's:
The cup is half full.
The alcoholic's:
The cup isn't big enough.

Wisdom *"He who guards his lips guards his life, but he who speaks rashly will come to ruin."*
— *Proverbs 13:3 (NIV)*

This is me ...
Everything that happens in my day is a learning experience. I watch for the lessons.

Journal

Date _____

Chuckle Q. How can we tell the difference between Sponsors and Therapist's?
A: Sponsors only use the word "closure," before the word mouth.

Wisdom *"Pride only breeds quarrels, but wisdom is found in those who take advice."*

— *Proverbs 13:10 (NIV)*

This is me ...
I do not feel that I am better or worse than anyone else.

Journal

Date _____

Chuckle Find an addict whose recovery books are falling apart from use, and I'll show you an addict who isn't.

Wisdom *"In the beginning was the Word, and the Word was with God, and the Word was God. He was with God in the beginning. Through him all things were made; without him nothing was made that has been made. In him was life, and that life was the light of men. The light shines in the darkness, but the darkness has not understood it."*

— *John 1:1-5 (NIV)*

This is me ...
I seek my Creator God where He has revealed Himself. I can find Him in His Word and in His creation.

Journal

Date _____

Chuckle A crack head walked up to a parking meter and put in a quarter. The arrow pointed to 60. "Will you look at that, he said. "I've lost 100 pounds!"

Wisdom _"A wise man fears the Lord and shuns evil, but a fool is hotheaded and reckless."_

— _Proverbs 13:16 (NIV)_

This is me ...
I don't gossip or speak badly about myself or others.

Journal

Date _____

Chuckle Did you hear about the addicts' "senility" disease? Everything is forgotten except the resentments.

Wisdom *"Whoever gives heed to instruction prospers, and blessed is he who trusts in the Lord."*

— Proverbs 16:20 (NIV)

This is me ...
I enjoy perpetual faith in my Creator God, in His love for me and in His deep desire that I live out His will for my life. This gives me a humble yet sound and realistic hope for the future. I am created in His image and likeness! His plans for me are beautiful.

Journal

Date _____

Chuckle In Recovery, it does not matter who is *right*—it only matters who is *left*.

Wisdom *"Avoiding danger is no safer in the long run than outright exposure. Life is either a daring adventure or nothing."*

— *Helen Keller*

This is me ...
I bounce out of bed nearly every morning because I know the day is going to be filled with exciting events and sweet success.

Journal

Date _____

Chuckle The sheriff of the local jail learned that a jug of home brew had been found. He sent this note to the inmates: "Roses are red, violets are blue, great try alkies, but you won't drink the brew."

The next morning he found this reply: "Dear Sheriff: 'Roses are red, violets are blue—you found one; we made two.

Wisdom *"Nothing is troublesome that we do willingly."*

— *Thomas Jefferson*

This is me ...
I love to laugh and have fun with whoever is near me each day.

Journal

Date _____

Chuckle Jim and Bob staggered down an alley between bars when a mugger pulled a gun and said, "Give me all your money." Both pulled out their wallets and started taking out their cash. Jim turned to Bob and gave him a bill and said, "Here's that $20 I owe you."

Wisdom _"If we do not change our direction, we are likely to end up where we are headed."_

— _Chinese proverb_

This is me ...
I am perfect where I am right now in my process of growth. This is where I am supposed to be on my journey toward my Father's home.

Journal

Date _____

Chuckle My drug use could be separated into three progressive stages: _impulsive_, _compulsive_ and _repulsive_.

Wisdom _"God asks no man whether he will accept life. That is not the choice. You must take it. The only choice is how."_

— Henry Ward Beecher

This is me ...
Every morning when I awaken I know that good things are going to happen to me and for me.

Journal

Date _____

Chuckle Jim Bob was swaying before the toilet and fumbling through his shirt pocket when a dollar fell out and landed right in the toilet. He thought for a minute wondering if a dollar was worth getting his hands in the water. Finally he took out a twenty dollar bill and threw it in with the one dollar bill and mumbled as he bent over to retrieve his money. "Twenty-one dollars is definitely worth going after!"

Wisdom _"God's gifts put man's best dreams to shame."_

— _Elizabeth Barrett Browning_

This is me ...
I am continually in the right place at the right time.

Journal

Date _____

Chuckle In July, those who come out with a fifth on the fourth often do not come forth on the fifth.

Wisdom *"In seeking happiness for others, you will find it in yourself."*
— *Unknown*

This is me ...
My life is an endless array of excitement and joy where I get to share love and laughter with the beautiful children of God. I am absolutely thrilled to be alive.

Journal

Date _____

Chuckle There was only $12 left of her paycheck when she got home late that night. Her husband started screaming at her about bills and responsibility. When he finished, the drunken wife slurred, "Well, at least I bought something for the house."

Smiling, he asked expectantly. "What was it?"

"A round of drinksh," she grinned.

Wisdom *"The lure of the distant and the difficult is deceptive. The great opportunity is where you are."*
— *John Burroughs*

This is me ...
My greatest blessings often come from what may seem to be my greatest challenges.

Journal

Chuckle After sitting up and worrying all night, the angry pre-Al Anon wife met her husband at the door. There was alcohol and pot on his breath, and his clothes were muddy, grass-stained and torn.

"I suppose that you have another lame excuse for coming home at five in the morning," she growled.

"Absolutely," he slurred back at her. "Breakfast."

Wisdom *"The mind grows by what it feeds on."*

— Josiah G. Holland

This is me ...
I read positive books and watch positive TV programs and movies. I become that which I feed my mind.

Journal

Date _____

Chuckle Every night a pothead came into her neighborhood pub and before ordering her a drink, would put her ear to the wall and listen silently. This went on for days until, finally, the bartender walked out from behind the bar, went over to the wall, put his ear to it. He listened for several minutes but heard nothing. So, he turned to the stoned lady and said, "I can't hear a thing." The lady shook her head and said, "Yeah, I know maaan. It's been like that for days!"

Wisdom _"Love your neighbor, yet pull not down your hedge."_

— George Herbert

This is me ...
Everything is temporary in this world except God. He is my permanent Master and Restorer. He is inexhaustibly sufficient.

Journal

Date _____

Chuckle Jim Bob was staggering down the street with a newspaper. A cop was following him and he noticed that every few steps, Jim Bob would tear off a piece of the paper and throw it out ahead of himself.

The cop finally stopped him and said, "Okay, buddy, what is going on with the paper throwing?"

Jim Bob replied, "I am chasing away the elephants!"

"Chasing elephants? There aren't any elephants in this city!" Said the cop.

Jim Bob answered, "Works pretty good, don't you think?"

Wisdom *"The heart at peace gives life to the body, but envy rots the bones."*
— *Proverbs 14:30 (NIV)*

This is me ...
I practice silence; this is an effective aid in achieving a peaceful mind. I turn off all noise and enjoy God's presence, which is always filled with love.

Journal

Date _____

Chuckle The hotel clerk was working graveyard shift. Shortly after three, the phone rang. Some drunk was asking what time the hotel lounge opened.

"It opens at noon," answered the clerk.

At four a.m. the same guy calls, only he is even more intoxicated.

"What time does the bar open?" The drunk asked.

"I told you—it opens at noon."

At five, he rings the clerk once again, only this time he is really plowed. "Whatdadjoooo shay the time openssh at the bar?"

Exasperated, The clerk said, "It opens at noon, but if you're in need of a drink now, I can have room service bring something up."

"No, no, no, joo donut undershhhand! I dooon wann in—I wann out!"

Wisdom _"The fear of the Lord is a fountain of life, turning a man from the snares of death."_

— _Proverbs 14:27 (NIV)_

This is me ...
I am relentless about keeping my thoughts and words positive and uplifting.

Journal

Date _____

Chuckle A doper slid up beside a stranger in the mall , saying, "Hey, man, have you got a few bucks that you can spare to help me feed my kids?"

"I don't think so," the stranger answered, "If I give you any money, you'll just spend it on drugs."

"No, I won't, I promise."

"And why should I believe you?"

"Because," whispered the red-eyed doper, "I've already got money for drugs!"

Wisdom _"If you have built castles in the air, your work need not be lost; that is where they should be. Now put foundations under them."_
— Henry David Thoreau

This is me ...
When a conversation seems to be heading in a negative or upsetting direction I try injecting peaceful, hopeful thoughts into it. Conversations filled with happy expectations and hope lift my soul and keep my mind focused on the light.

Journal

Date _____

Chuckle The police officer had just handed him a ticket, but the crack-head was belligerent. "What am I supposed to do with this?" He demanded.

"Keep it," the police officer replied. "When you collect three of them, you get a bicycle."

Wisdom _"The only ones among you who will be really happy are those who will have sought and found how to serve."_

— _Albert Schweitzer_

This is me ...
I have the heart of a servant. Serving God and others brings me joy.

Journal

Date _____

Chuckle Two speed freaks were walking at a brisk pace along the railroad track when one of them impatiently complained to the other, "I sure wish we'd get to the bottom of this flight of stairs."

"The stairs aren't the hardest part of it," argued the second bright-eyed speeder. "It's the low handrail that is killing me."

Wisdom _"A cheerful look brings joy to the heart, and good news gives health to the bones."_

— _Proverbs 15:30 (NIV)_

This is me ...
I become as innocent as a child and as wise as any man, when I sit quietly in God's presence and listen.

Journal

Date _____

Chuckle Q: How many glue sniffers does it take to change a light bulb? A: Just one. He can hold the bulb in place and let the room spin around.

Wisdom *"How much better to get wisdom than gold, to choose understanding rather than silver!"*
— *Proverbs 16:16 (NIV)*

This is me ...
I gain wisdom and understanding through every experience.

_____

_____

_____

_____

_____

_____

_____

_____

_____

_____

_____

_____

_____

_____

_____

_____

_____

_____

_____

_____

_____

_____

Journal

Chuckle Jim Bob got a job selling vacuum cleaners. He approached a farm house and when the lady answered the door he pushed his way into her living room and threw some horse manure on the floor, saying, "Madam, thank you for allowing me to demonstrate

the world's best vacuum cleaner. I'm so confident that our vacuum will clean anything, I promise I will eat every bit of that horse manure it doesn't pick up."

"Well, I sure hope you're hungry," she replied, "because we don't have electricity."

Wisdom _"The highway of the upright avoids evil; he who guards his way guards his life."_

— _Proverbs 16:17 (NIV)_

This is me ...
I will not surrender the freedom of choice my Creator has granted me in exchange for being a slave to addictions and character defects again. Therefore, I will stay grounded by actively using the 12 Steps of recovery in all my affairs.

Journal

Date _____

Chuckle Jim Bob was staggering down the road and thumbing for a ride. A kind man stopped his car. Jim Bob got in, stinking of gin. After they'd been riding a minute or two, Jim Bob noticed a brown bag full of booze on the front seat. "What's in the bag?" He asked.

"It's a bottle of wine. I got it for my wife," the driver replied.

Jim Bob sat silent for another minute, then said, "Good trade."

Wisdom *"Now faith is being sure of what we hope for and certain of what we do not see."*

— *Hebrews 11:1 (NIV)*

This is me ...
I receive exactly what I need.

Journal

Date _____

Chuckle Mother: "Yes, honey, your father is finally going to AA."

Daughter: "But Mom, I saw him stumbling out of the Oasis Tavern this morning. He was even drunker than he usually is."

Mother: "I know, darlin', but he's drinking under an assumed name, now."

Wisdom _"You have heard the law that says, 'Love your neighbor' and hate your enemy. But I say, love your enemies! Pray for those who persecute you! In that way, you will be acting as true children of your Father in heaven. For he gives his sunlight to both the evil and the good, and he sends rain on the just and the unjust alike."_

— Matthew 5:43-45 (NLT)

This is me ...
I regularly complete the most unpleasant task first. Then, I'm no longer anxious about it. This makes the rest of what I have to do more pleasant.

Journal

Date _____

Chuckle Jim and Bob were having a typical drunk conversation:
Jim: "Hey, Bob, I heard that you started a band."
Bob: "Yeah, man, we rock n' roll, baby!"
Jim: "How many are in the band, man?"
Bob: "There are three of us, dude."
Jim: "Three?"
Bob: "Yeah, me and my brother."
Jim: "You have a brother, man?"
Bob: "No, why do you ask?"

Wisdom _"If you would be loved, love, and be lovable."_

— _Benjamin Franklin_

This is me ...
I live in a timeless environment because I live in the moment. I do not wander into the future with its worries and fears.
I do not revisit the resentments and regrets of the past. I participate fully in this moment because this is where my God can be found.

Journal

Date _____

Chuckle Jim Bob was eating at the soup kitchen when he had to go to the bathroom.
He didn't want anyone to take his soup while he was gone so he took a napkin and wrote: "I have spit in this soup." When he returned someone else had written: "Me, too."

Wisdom *"Today, if you hear His voice, do not harden your hearts as you did in the rebellion."*

— *Hebrews 3:15 (NIV)*

This is me ...
I listen for God's voice, His still, small voice. For—He is my Teacher.

Journal

Date _____

Chuckle There are only two potentially dangerous times in sobriety as far as the possibility of relapse is concerned. One is during the first thirty days. The other is any time after that.

Wisdom *"Even though I was once a blasphemer and a persecutor and a violent man, I was shown mercy because I acted in ignorance and unbelief. The grace of our Lord was poured out on me abundantly, along with the faith and love that are in Christ Jesus."*

1 Timothy 1:13-14 (NIV)

This is me ...
When I am tempted to think about or to do something I know is wrong, I can trust that God has provided a way out. The surest way out, is to simply focus my mind on something else.
If I try to overcome the temptation, I often lose the battle.
I seek God's direction and guidance as He renews my mind.
I can simply change what I am thinking about to something positive—like His presence, a happy place, a memorized prayer or bible verse. When I do this, the temptation simply fades away and eventually stops returning. The brain God gave me dissolves unused thought patterns. This never fails—if practiced long enough.

Journal

Date _____

Chuckle After stopping by his partner's pad for a few too many bong hits, the old hippie was driving down the interstate. He was pokin' along when his cell phone rang. It was his ol' lady who was freakin' out. She screamed frantically, "Wow, honey, be careful coming home. I just heard on the news that there is a car driving the wrong way on the interstate!"

"Maaan," said the old stoner, "It's not just one—they're all going the wrong way!"

Wisdom _"People are lonely because they build walls instead of bridges."_
— _Joseph Fort Newton_

This is me ...
I keep my life in balance between worship, work and play. I need all three to be a healthy me.

Journal

Date _____

Chuckle A teenaged girl tried sneaking in the back door after being out drinking till three a.m. Her dad, however, was waiting up and caught her coming in. "Where have you been all night, young lady?" He demanded.

"Oh, hi, daddy. I was over at Jenny's."

"You know you're not to be drinking, and you are not to be out this late," growled the upset father.

"Well, I uh, had some car trouble, Dad."

"Car trouble! What kind of car trouble?"

The teen stood there thoughtfully for a moment and said, "Water in the motor."

"What! Water in the motor! It hasn't rained for weeks! Where's the car now?"

Staring her Dad straight in the eye, she replied, "In Jenny's swimming pool."

Wisdom *"You grow up the day you have the first real laugh—at yourself."*
— *Ethel Barrymore*

This is me ...
I take responsibility for my choices. My Father God has given me free will which I use as I choose. I choose to seek His will. Then I am truly free.

Journal

Chuckle Jim and Bob were stranded on an island for years when Jim came upon a magical lamp on the beach. He rubbed it and sure enough, out came a genie who offers to grant them each one wish. "Jim says: "I want off this island," and he immediately vanishes. Bob says: "I can't decide. I wish Jim was here to help me."

Wisdom *"The precepts of the Lord are right, giving joy to the heart. The commands of the Lord are radiant, giving light to the eyes."*

-- Psalms 19:8 NIV

This is me ...
I will seek to discover and understand the precepts of the Lord, for in them I will find joy for my heart and light for my eyes.

Journal

Date _____

Chuckle Drinking doesn't drown my sorrows; it irrigates them.

Wisdom _"Then God said, 'Let us make man in our image, in our likeness, and let them rule over the fish of the sea and the birds of the air, over the livestock, over all the earth, and over all the creatures that move along the ground.' So God created man in his own image, in the image of God he created him; male and female he created them."_

— _Genesis 1:26-27 (NIV)_

This is me ...
I am the most valuable piece of functional art this side of heaven. I consist of over 100 trillion individual cells. If it were even possible for man to do it, it would cost billions and billions and billions and billions and billions of dollars to make—me.
I am the only me there will ever be.
I am valuable beyond my ability to comprehend treasure. My Creator and Redeemer not only made me, but paid an even greater price to rescue me from this troubled world. His desire to be with me forever is inexhaustible.

Journal

Date _____

Chuckle When I go to one meeting a week, I can stay clean. When I go to two meetings a week, I enjoy being clean. When I go to at least three meetings a week, other people start to act better!

Wisdom _"You are worthy, our Lord and God, to receive glory and honor and power, for you created all things, and by your will they were created and have their being."_

— _Revelation 4:11 (NIV)_

This is me ...
I have and endless supply of money because I use my God's principles for handling it.
I recognize that everything in the world is His, including all the money He gives me the ability to earn.
I do this by gratefully returning the correct amount to Him, through good charities, as tithe. I serve Him—not money. I try to use the money He gives me in noble ways. This often involves freely sharing it with others in need.

Journal

Date _____

Chuckle When Jim Bob showed up late for work again, his boss yelled: "You should have been here at 8:00!" Jim Bob replied, "Why, what happened at 8:00?"

Wisdom _"But for Adam no suitable helper was found. So the LORD God caused the man to fall into a deep sleep; and while he was sleeping, he took one of the man's ribs and closed up the place with flesh. Then the Lord God made a woman from the rib he had taken out of the man, and he brought her to the man."_
— _Genesis 2:20-22 (NIV)_

This is me ...
I am attentive to my mate here on earth. The intimacy and joy-filled closeness of our relationship is without match in this world. May my mate know, without a doubt, how completely and utterly committed I am to the gift of our union.

Journal

Date _____

Chuckle Q: How many Al-Anons does it take to change a light bulb? A: Three: One to make coffee, one to chair, and one to guide it through the Steps so it can learn to change itself.

Wisdom *"He redeemed my soul from going down to the pit and I will live to enjoy the light. God does all these things to a man—twice, even three times—to turn back his soul from the pit, that the light of life may shine on him.'"*
— Job 33:28-29 (NIV)

This is me ...
God gives me the exact training, experience and gifts I need to be who I am, so I can fulfill His purposes for my life.

Journal

Date _____

Chuckle Jim Bob was arguing with a friend in recovery about going to meetings. He finally said, "No, I don't need to go to meetings because, unlike you, I am only an alcoholic when I drink."

Wisdom *"'Be just and fair to all,' says the LORD. 'Do what is right and good, for I am coming soon to rescue you. Blessed are those who are careful to do this. Blessed are those who honor my Sabbath days of rest by refusing to work. And blessed are those who keep themselves from doing wrong.'"*
— *Isaiah 56:1-2 (NLT)*

This is me ...
My hopes and dreams are becoming reality today because I am clean and sober and seeking the will of my Creator.

Journal

Chuckle A new game was invented to be played at Al anon meetings. It's called, "Pin the Blame on the Jackass."

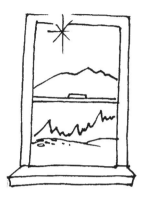

Wisdom *"The Lord is my light and my salvation—whom shall I fear? The Lord is the stronghold of my life—of whom shall I be afraid?"*

— Psalm 27:1 (NIV)

This is me ...
I stand in awe of the magnificent, timeless, boundless, measureless, inexhaustible love of my Creator God.

Journal

Chuckle Jim Bob was staggering down the sidewalk in an elegant neighborhood when a snooty woman walked up to him and said, "Sir, you are drunk." Jim Bob replied, "Madam, you are ugly. But I have hope, for in the morning, I will be sober."

Wisdom *"Argue for your limitations, and sure enough, they're yours."*

— *Richard Bach*

This is me ...
I strive to arrive on time for appointments because other people are so important to me.

Journal

Date _____

Chuckle Jim and Bob were hiking in Hells Canyon when Bob was suddenly bit by a rattlesnake right in the butt.

Jim said, "Don't worry, I'll climb to the top of the canyon and use my cell phone to call a Doctor for advice."

The doctor told Jim to make a small cut over the spot where the snake bite was and suck out the venom.

Jim rushed back to Bob's side and said: "I'm so sorry, man. The Doctor says you're not going to make it."

Wisdom _"'I know that my Redeemer lives, and that in the end he will stand upon the earth. And after my skin has been destroyed, yet in my flesh I will see God; I myself will see him with my own eyes—I, and not another. How my heart yearns within me!'"_

— Job 19:25-27 (NIV)

This is me ...
My curiosity and joy at discovering the endless adventures of life are limitless.

Journal

Date _____

Chuckle Acronyms:
DENIAL: Don't Even Notice I Am Lying.
HOPE: Hearing Other People's
Experience.
ISM: I Sponsor Myself.

Wisdom _"'For God so loved the world
that he gave his one and only Son,
that whoever believes in him shall not
perish but have eternal life.
For God did not send his Son into the
world to condemn the world, but to
save the world through him.'"_
— John 3:16-17 (NIV)

This is me ...
As I give my will and life to my Father
God, He takes my hand and leads me
into the light. I am so very grateful that
He provided a way for me to get home.
He is the Way and the Truth and the
Life.

Journal

Date _____

Chuckle As a woman was leaving a store, a half-baked stoner grabbed her purse and ran. Within 10 minutes, the police caught him, put him in the car, and drove him back to the store. The stoner was told to stand in front of the woman for a positive identification.

To this, he replied, "Yea, maaan, that's her—that's the lady I stole the purse from."

Wisdom _"'Therefore I tell you, do not worry about your life, what you will eat or drink; or about your body, what you will wear. Is not life more important than food, and the body more important than clothes? Look at the birds of the air; they do not sow or reap or store away in barns, and yet your heavenly Father feeds them. Are you not much more valuable than they? Who of you by worrying can add a single hour to his life?'"_

— _Matthew 6:25-34 (NIV)_

This is me ...
I never worry because I have released the direction and care of my life into the hands of my Father God. I trust Him completely and know perfect peace.

Journal

Date _____

Chuckle Jim and Bob both made their own beer. They always argued over whose was the best. Finally, they agreed to send a sample of their beers off to the National Center for Beer Tasting to get an impartial, scientific opinion as to which beer was the best. After a month they got the report back: "We are sorry to inform you that both of your cows have diabetes."

Wisdom _"Who has woe? Who has sorrow? Who has strife? Who has complaints? Who has needless bruises? Who has bloodshot eyes? Those who linger over wine, who go to sample bowls of mixed wine. Do not gaze at wine when it is red, when it sparkles in the cup, when it goes down smoothly! In the end it bites like a snake and poisons like a viper. Your eyes will see strange sights and your mind imagine confusing things. You will be like one sleeping on the high seas, lying on top of the rigging. 'They hit me,' you will say, 'but I'm not hurt! They beat me, but I don't feel it! When will I wake up so I can find another drink?'"_
— _Proverbs 23:29-35 (NIV)_

This is me ...
I never have to return to the nightmare of addiction again, because my Father God is now the director of my affairs.

Journal

Date _____

Chuckle Two drunks were driving down a country road one day when they came up behind a horse trailer. As they got closer they could see there was something written on the trailer below the horses' rear ends. It read, "Don't be what you are looking at."

Wisdom _"He whose walk is blameless is kept safe, but he whose ways are perverse will suddenly fall."_

— _Proverbs 28:18 (NIV)_

This is me ...
My walk is blameless for God is directing my thinking and my actions. I am entirely surrendered to His will.

Journal

Date _____

Chuckle An evangelist was preaching against the evils of alcohol. At the end of his sermon he said, "If I had all of the beer in the world, I would throw it in the river. And if I had all of the wine in the world, I would take it and throw it in the river. And if I had all of the hard liquor in the world, I would throw it in the river." Then he took a seat. The choir leader had the congregation stand, and with his head bowed he said, "Let's sing our closing hymn: 'Shall we gather at the river?'"

Wisdom _"It is through the pen that we discover the light."_

— _Linda T., La Grande, Oregon_

This is me ...
I ask God to reveal His will as I write in my journal.

Journal

Chuckle Jim Bob, at the wheel of a ship at night, saw a light dead ahead approaching fast on a collision course. He sent the signal: "Change your course ten degrees east!"

The light signaled back: "Change yours, ten degrees west!"

Jim Bob got angry and sent: "I'm a Navy Captain! Change your course, sir!"

Reply: "I'm a Seaman, Second Class. Change your course!"

Jim Bob, furious now: "I'm a battleship! I'm not changing course!"

And the final reply: "I'm a lighthouse. Your call."

Wisdom *"All hard work brings a profit, but mere talk leads only to poverty."*

— *Proverbs 14:23 (NIV)*

This is me ...
I am attractive to and admired by people, because I am loving, kind and have an enjoyable attitude.

Journal

Date _____

Chuckle Two stoners were talking as they finished a bowl:

First stoner: You want to go for a walk?

Second stoner: No, it's windy?

First stoner: No, it's Thursday.

Second stoner: Me, too. Let's get a beer!

Wisdom *"Most people repent their sins by thanking God they ain't so wicked as their neighbors."*

— *Josh Billings*

This is me ...
I desire to fill my heart and mind with good positive information and happy healthy entertainment.

Journal

Date _____

Chuckle Jim and Bob were out for a round of golf one day. Suddenly, a funeral procession passed by. Jim pulled off his cap, placed it over his heart, bowed his head and actually shed a tear as the procession passed. Touched, Bob said: "Wow, Jim, I never knew that you were such a sensitive person. You are truly kind hearted." Yeah, well," Jim replied, "we were married for 30 years."

Wisdom _"Fear is the dark room where negatives are developed."_

— _Anonymous_

This is me ...
Tranquility and serenity are my perennial companions. I walk in God's love and light.

Journal

Date _____

Chuckle "Adversity is the only diet that will reduce a fat head."

— *Jacob Braude*

Wisdom *"Experience is not what happens to you, it is what you do with what happens to you."*

— *Aldous Huxley*

This is me ...
The will of God is the all-absorbing purpose of my life.

Journal

Date _____

Chuckle You can't fall out of bed if you sleep on the floor.

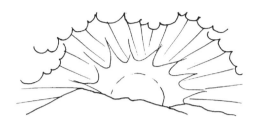

Wisdom _"In the beginning God created the heavens and the earth. Now the earth was formless and empty, darkness was over the surface of the deep, and the Spirit of God was hovering over the waters. And God said, 'Let there be light,' and there was light. God saw that the light was good, and he separated the light from the darkness. God called the light 'day,' and the darkness he called 'night.' And there was evening, and there was morning—the first day."_

— _Genesis 1:1-3 (NIV)_

This is me ...
Nothing insures my immunity from relapse in a more powerful way than intensive work with others who suffer.

Journal

Date _____

Chuckle "I can resist everything except temptation."

— _Oscar Wilde_

Wisdom _"You are what you are when no one is looking."_

— _Robert C. Edwards_

This is me ...
Each right decision carried out in spite of difficulties makes my character stronger and my walk with my Creator closer.

Journal

Date _____

Chuckle After smoking one too many bowls, a half-baked young lady was walking beside the river. Suddenly, her friend who was on the other side of the water spotted her and yelled out, "Hey, Susan, how do I get on the other side of the river?" Susan thought for a moment and with a bewildered look she yelled back, "You are on the other side of the river!"

Wisdom _"A cheerful heart is good medicine, but a crushed spirit dries up the bones."_

— _Proverbs 17:22 (NIV)_

This is me ...
I understand the connection between health and wholeness. That is why I eat right, exercise, drink lots of pure water, get plenty of rest, sunshine and fresh air.
It is also why I feed my mind happy, healthy entertainment and uplifting, loving thoughts.

Journal

Date _____

Chuckle Jim Bob had landed in the nut house again where they were trying to dry him out. As he was walking down the hall a fellow patient stepped out of his room wearing nothing but a pair of fake pistols and a gun belt. He said to Jim Bob, "Hold it right there mister, I am going to blow your head off."

"Who are you?" Jim Bob inquired.

"I am Wyatt Earp," the fellow yelled back, "and I am going to blow your head clean off."

"Who told you that you were Wyatt Earp?" Jim Bob asked.

"God did," he replied.

Suddenly, another patient in the room yelled out, "I did not."

Wisdom *"No man can think clearly when his fists are clenched."*

— *George Jean Nathan*

This is me ...
My love is revealed in doing God's will.

Journal

Date _____

Chuckle Give an alcoholic a fish and he will eat for a day. Teach an alcoholic to fish and he will sit by a lake and drink beer for the rest of his life.

Wisdom *"A man of knowledge uses words with restraint, and a man of understanding is even-tempered."*
— *Proverbs 17:27 (NIV)*

This is me ...
God gives me opportunities; I am successful because I prepare for and take advantage of those opportunities when they arrive.

Journal

Date _____

Chuckle "I feel sorry for people who don't drink or do drugs. Because some day they are going to be lying in a hospital bed, dying, and they won't know why."

— Redd Foxx

Wisdom _"Since you call on a Father who judges each man's work impartially, live your lives as strangers here in reverent fear. For you know that it was not with perishable things such as silver or gold that you were redeemed from the empty way of life handed down to you from your forefathers, but with the precious blood of Christ, a lamb without blemish or defect."_

— 1 Peter 1:17-19 (NIV)

This is me ...
I no longer put poisons into my body.
I strive to live in harmony with all people.
I have turned my will and life over to the care of my loving Father God.

Journal

Chuckle "Cheer up, the worst is yet to come."

— *Philander Johnson*

Wisdom *"Even a fool is thought wise if he keeps silent, and discerning if he holds his tongue."*

— *Proverbs 17:28 (NIV)*

This is me ...
I consciously bring uplifting comments to all conversations.

Journal

Date _____

Chuckle "We ought never to do wrong when people are looking."
— _Mark Twain_

Wisdom _"In the way of righteousness there is life; along that path is immortality."_
— _Proverbs 12:28 (NIV)_

This is me ...
I fully experience and hold precious every perfect moment of my life.
I find joy even in the midst of my most difficult struggles.

Journal

Chuckle Jim Bob staggered into a bar and ordered a drink. "I'm sorry," said the bartender, "I can't serve you unless you are wearing a tie."

Jim Bob staggered back out to his car, opened his trunk, grabbed a pair of jumper cables, wrapped them around his neck and staggered back into the bar.

"How do you like this here tie?"

"Well, okay, sir," replied the bartender, "but don't start anything."

Wisdom *"Courage faces fear and thereby masters it."*

— *Martin Luther King, Jr.*

This is me ...
When I keep my body mind and spirit in the best possible condition, I am better able to resist the temptations that seek to destroy my soul.

Journal

Date _____

Chuckle Jim Bob was celebrating his 15th birthday in N.A. A newcomer came up to him after the meeting and asked how he managed to stay clean for so long. Jim Bob replied, "I trust God, clean house, serve others, I don't take drugs, no matter what and I never argue with anyone." The newcomer couldn't believe it, he said, "That's impossible! There has to be more to it than that!" Jim Bob just smiled at him and said, "Maybe you're right."

Wisdom _"But now a righteousness from God, apart from the law, has been made known, to which the Law and the Prophets testify. This righteousness from God comes through faith in Jesus Christ to all who believe. There is no difference, for all have sinned and fall short of the glory of God, and are justified freely by his grace through the redemption that came by Christ Jesus."_
— _Romans 3:21-24 (NIV)_

This is me ...
I trust God, clean house, serve others, never drink or do drugs and argue with no one.

Journal

Date _____

Chuckle "The worst thing about the opposite sex is that when they're not drunk, they're sober."

— *W. B. Yeats*

Wisdom *"Wine is a mocker and beer a brawler; whoever is lead astray by them is not wise."*

— *Proverbs 20:1 (NIV)*

This is me ...
I have a firm grasp on the direction of my life because I have a well proven written plan for how to manage it each day—The Twelve Steps.

_____

_____

_____

_____

_____

_____

_____

_____

Journal

Date _____

Chuckle "An alcoholic is someone you don't like who drinks as much as you do."
— _Dylan Thomas_

Wisdom _"A gentle answer turns away wrath, but a harsh word stirs up anger."_
— _Proverbs 15:1 (NIV)_

This is me ...
People like me because I'm so fun to be with.

Journal

Date _____

Chuckle Four clergymen were sharing their personal addiction issues.

The first said, "I drink too much; sometimes I drink in the morning just to get my day started."

The second said, "Sometimes I steal the week's offerings and go to the horse track to gamble."

The third said, "I often have had sex with the lonely women in my congregation."

The fourth minister said, "I can relate to all of you, only my problem is that I am addicted to gossip."

Wisdom *"All of a man's ways seem innocent to him but motives are weighed by the Lord."*

— Proverbs 16:2 (NIV)

This is me ...
I feel good about myself because I have found the place I fit best in the whole world—being me!

Journal

Date _____

Chuckle Why join AA when you already have a good towing service?

Wisdom *"When a man's ways are pleasing to the Lord, he makes even his enemies live at peace with him."*
— *Proverbs 16:7 (NIV)*

This is me ...
A great teacher never strives to explain his vision. He simply invites you to stand along side and see for yourself.
— *R. Inman*

Journal

Date _____

Chuckle Prior to AA the only way a family in Ireland could get rid of an alcoholic was to buy them a one-way ticket to America.

Wisdom _"In his heart a man plans his course, but the Lord determines his steps."_

— _Proverbs 16:9 (NIV)_

This is me ...
Prayer is my constant activity. I lean not on my own moral power but seek God's power. As I do this with complete abandon, I no longer vacillate between principle and inclination.

Journal

Date _____

Chuckle A pot-head called his friend one night about midnight, he was extremely agitated.

"Get over here right away," he yelled in a panic, "it's a real emergency! And bring some pot with you."

The friend raced across town with his bag and bowl, ran into the house and blurted, "Wow, man what's up! I was freakin out all the way here."

"I'm broke and out of pot. maaan. Thanks for comin'."

Wisdom _"The tongue that brings healing is a tree of life, but a deceitful tongue crushes the spirit."_
— _Proverbs 15:4 (NIV)_

This is me ...
I can, because I think I can.

Journal

Date _____

Chuckle While in the army, Jim Bob would constantly walk around picking up pieces of paper. He would then get angry and throw it to the ground and scowl, "That ain't it."

His commanding officer finally sent him in for an evaluation where the shrink determined that he was unfit for duty and they awarded him a medical discharge. As the officer gave him his paperwork, he smiled and said, "Oh, there it is!"

Wisdom _"A fool finds no pleasure in understanding but delights in airing his own opinions."_

— _Proverbs 18:2 (NIV)_

This is me ...
I will never stop learning.

Journal

Date _____

Chuckle After long and solemn consideration and many hours of deep meditation, Jim and Bob decided to stop smoking pot. They were even going to go to church and tell the pastor of their awesome decision.

On the way there Jim said, "Hey, maaan, before we get to church to tell the pastor that we are done forever, lets smoke one last victory bowl."

Bob said, "No, maaan, the pastor will smell it on us; lets smoke it on the way back, dude!"

"Oh, yeah, maaan. Duuuhhh," replied Jim, "what was I thinking?"

Wisdom _"The Lord detests the thoughts of the wicked, but those of the pure are pleasing to him."_
— _Proverbs 15:26 (NIV)_

This is me ...
I remain true to God and He rewards me with exceptional wisdom and insight.

Journal

Date _____

Chuckle Jim Bob was riding on a bus when a woman got on who was holding a baby. The bus driver said: "That is the ugliest baby that I have ever seen!"

She walks to the back of the bus where Jim Bob is sipping on a jug and tells him, "That bus driver just insulted me."

Jim Bob slurs. "You go right up there and tell him off! Go ahead! I'll hold your monkey for you."

Wisdom _"He who loves pleasure will become poor; whoever loves wine and oil will never be rich."_

— _Proverbs 21:17 (NIV)_

This is me ...
My heavenly Father God loves me without reservations or conditions. He is a perfect Father.

Journal

Date _____

Chuckle The wise old Doctor told his suffering patient, "If you just stop drinking, you will live longer."

"If I quit drinking, I may or may not live any longer, Doc," the patient replied, "but it will certainly seem that way."

Wisdom _"Therefore, since Christ suffered in his body, arm yourselves also with the same attitude, because he who has suffered in his body is done with sin._

As a result, he does not live the rest of his earthly life for evil human desires, but rather for the will of God. For you have spent enough time in the past doing what pagans choose to do—living in debauchery, lust, drunkenness, orgies, carousing and detestable idolatry."

— 1 Peter 4:1-3 (NIV)

This is me ...
God persistently draws my heart away from evil and into His wonderfully exciting and fulfilling presence.

Journal

Date _____

Chuckle "The best thing for you," said the doctor to Jim Bob, "is to give up drinking, doing drugs, smoking, and wild women."

Jim Bob thought for a moment, then asked, "What's the next best thing?"

Wisdom *"A friend loves at all times, and a brother is born for a time of adversity."*

— Proverbs 17:17 (NIV)

This is me ...
I continue to grow mentally, spiritually and emotionally.
Those who are not busy being born are busy dying.
I am busy being born.

Journal

Date _____

Chuckle An addict or alcoholic is someone who buys a bottle of one-a-day vitamins and immediately takes two. When he sees a sign over the bar that says "All you can drink, $5.00," he puts down a ten-dollar bill, just in case.

Wisdom *"'For I know the plans I have for you,' says the LORD, 'They are plans for good and not for disaster, to give you a future and a hope. In those days when you pray, I will listen.'"*
— Jeremiah 29:11-12 (NLT)

This is me ...
I'm excited about where I'm headed because God directs my paths.

_____

_____

_____

_____

_____

_____

_____

_____

_____

_____

_____

_____

_____

Journal

Chuckle It was 30 below zero one blistering winter night. Jim Bob was sitting on his usual bar stool sipping his drink. The bartender came up to him with his tab and said, "Look, Jim Bob, you're past due on your bar tab. I'm going to need some kind of collateral if you are going to keep drinking. I am also going to write your name here on the wall beside the amount you owe until you get me paid up."

"No," Jim Bob cried in horror, "I don't want all my friends to know that!"

"Don't worry Jim Bob, no one will know," replied the bartender. "I'll just hang your coat over it until it's paid!"

Wisdom *"Those who live according to the sinful nature have their minds set on what that nature desires; but those who live in accordance with the Spirit have their minds set on what the Spirit desires. The mind of sinful man is death, but the mind controlled by the Spirit is life and peace; the sinful mind is hostile to God. It does not submit to God's law, nor can it do so. Those controlled by the sinful nature cannot please God."*

— *Romans 8:5-8 (NIV)*

This is me ...
I walk without fear because I trust my Father God with every step I take.

Journal

Date _____

Chuckle After staggering to his car and fumbling with his keys a long while, Jim Bob was approached by a police officer who said, "Now, surely, sir, you're not really thinking of driving a car, considering the awful shape you're in?"

"I certainly am," replied Jim Bob. "You don't expect me to walk in this condition, do you?"

Wisdom _"Then he said, 'Beware! Don't be greedy for what you don't have. Real life is not measured by how much we own.'"_

— Luke 12:15 (NLT)

This is me ...
I make amends promptly after I have done something wrong, if I don't cause more harm in doing so. This sets my soul free and their soul free.

Journal

Date _____

Chuckle A new employee stood before the paper shredder looking confused. Jim Bob stumbled by and asked, "Need some help?"

"Yes," she replied, "how does this thing work?"

"Simple," Jim Bob replied. He took her papers and fed them into the shredder. "There you are," he said.

She asked, "But where do the copies come out?"

Wisdom _"The LORD is my light and my salvation—so why should I be afraid? The LORD protects me from danger—so why should I tremble?"_

— _Psalm 27:1-2 (NLT)_

This is me ...
Sometimes I worry about things, then I remember that God is in complete control.
I relax and find peace in trusting Him.

Journal

Date _____

Chuckle A teenager came home after a couple of hours spent drinking with her friends. As she fell through the doorway, her father snapped at her. "What is wrong with you young lady? How dare you come home half-drunk!"

"I'm sorry, Dad," the teen replied, "we ran out of booze."

Wisdom _"'And this is my covenant with them,' says the LORD. 'My Spirit will not leave them, and neither will these words I have given you. They will be on your lips and on the lips of your children and your children's children forever. I, The LORD, have spoken!'"_
— _Isaiah 59:21 (NLT}_

This is me ...
There is joy in every moment of life, I will seek it. I will find it in knowing that God is with me.

Journal

Date _____

Chuckle Jim Bob was up late one night drinking and watching the Home Shopping Network. He finally called them and they answered: "Good evening, may we help you?"

"No," replied Jim Bob, "I just looking."

Wisdom _"For the word of God is living and active. Sharper than any double-edged sword, it penetrates even to dividing soul and spirit, joints and marrow; it judges the thoughts and attitudes of the heart. Nothing in all creation is hidden from God's sight. Everything is uncovered and laid bare before the eyes of him to whom we must give account."_

Hebrews 4:11-12 (NIV)

This is me ...
I give myself positive feedback about who I am.
I am God's child.
I will continually reinforce the thought that I am beautiful internally and externally, and successful in every area of my life.

Journal

Date _____

Chuckle Words, defined by an alcoholic:
Monday: A sick day.
Wagon: Not drinking for 24 hours in a row.
Abstinence: Drinking only after noon.
Self-discipline: Leaving some beer in the bottom of a glass.
Barroom: Conference room, loan office, dating service, counseling center, answering service, sports arena.
Alcoholic: The person on the stool next to yours."

Wisdom _"Truth stands the test of time; lies are soon exposed."_
— _Proverbs 12:19 (NLT)_

This is me ...
I am not reluctant to show my feelings. When I am happy I show it. When things are tough I can turn to my partners in recovery and share honestly.

Journal

Date _____

Chuckle: Jim Bob was staggering down an alley carrying a box. Two other winos came up to him to see what he had.

"What ya got in the box Jim Bob?"

"It's a mongoose. I got him to chase away the snakes I see when I have hallucinations."

"Jim Bob, you're an idiot, man, those snakes aren't real."

"That's OK," responded Jim Bob, "neither is the mongoose."

Wisdom *"'Don't store up treasures here on earth, where they can be eaten by moths and get rusty, and where thieves break in and steal. Store your treasures in heaven, where they will never become moth-eaten or rusty and where they will be safe from thieves. Wherever your treasure is, there your heart and thoughts will also be.'"*

— Matthew 6:19-21 (NLT}

This is me ...
I set aside time every day to practice the presence of God. I know that He is always there. I love being with Him.

Journal

Date _____

Chuckle Bored sitting at home alone every day, drinking, a woman alcoholic decided to take up horse back riding. One day while staggering down the road, she spotted a horse all saddled up and ready to go. Deciding to give it a try, she jumped right on the thing. It was going well for a moment, but then the horse started to gallop. Soon she was sliding off the side of the beast. The next thing she knew, she was hanging upside down around his neck. Realizing she was about to be trampled, she decided to fling herself off to the side. But as she did, her foot got caught in the stirrup. As she bounced along, her head was being pounded against the ground, she started to pass out, thinking this is the bitter end. However, to her good fortune, the Walmart manager came over and unplugged the carousel.

Wisdom _"Be not afraid of growing slowly. Be afraid only of standing still."_
— Chinese proverb

This is me ...
I am humbly intelligent, I look great and feel great.
I am happy, joyous and free.

Journal

Date _____

Chuckle A long-winded newcomer to NA was sharing his experience from the podium. He got carried away and talked for two hours.

Finally, he realized what he was doing and said, "I'm sorry I talked so long. I left my watch at home."

An old timer called out from the back of the room, "There's a calendar right behind you."

Wisdom _"When the fight begins within himself, a man is worth something."_

— Robert Frost

This is me ...
"I am a glorious being. A miracle. That which is in God is also in me. I survive all storms, and like a tree planted by the water, I shall not be moved."

— Susan L. Taylor

Journal

Chuckle After a long relapse an old hippie comes back to his group one night, completely wasted. The greeter at the door warned him, "You had better give it up, maaan! I'd hate to come to your funeral!"

The old hippie replies, "Hey, maaan, I didn't invite you."

Wisdom *"But although the world was made through him, the world didn't recognize him when he came. Even in his own land and among his own people, he was not accepted. But to all who believed him and accepted him, he gave the right to become children of God. They are reborn! This is not a physical birth resulting from human passion or plan—this rebirth comes from God.*

So the Word became human and lived here on earth among us. He was full of unfailing love and faithfulness. And we have seen his glory, the glory of the only Son of the Father."
— *John 1:10-14 (NLT)*

This is me ...
I have been reborn through the grace of my wonderful Father God.
I am completely new.

Journal

Date _____

Chuckle Jim Bob staggered into a bar, seated himself slowly on a stool, and asked for something to drink in a hurry. The bartender began suggesting different types of drinks but Jim Bob said, "Just give me something fast, that is loaded with alcohol." The man sitting on the next stool turned and slurred indignantly, "Sir, you are talking about the woman I love!"

Wisdom _"The acts of the sinful nature are obvious: sexual immorality, impurity and debauchery; idolatry and witchcraft; hatred, discord, jealousy, fits of rage, selfish ambition, dissensions, factions and envy; drunkenness, orgies, and the like. I warn you, as I did before, that those who live like this will not inherit the kingdom of God._

But the fruit of the Spirit is love, joy, peace, patience, kindness, goodness, faithfulness, gentleness and self-control. Against such things there is no law. Those who belong to Christ Jesus have crucified the sinful nature its passions and desires.

Since we live by the Spirit, let us keep in step with the Spirit. Let us not become conceited, provoking and envying each other."

— Galatians 5:19-26 (NIV)

This is me ...
I never rob myself of peace and serenity by drinking in or pouring out anger and resentment. I am free.

Journal

Date _____

Chuckle One night, a pastor was working late when he heard a knock at his door. There in the dark stood Jim Bob, completely smashed.

"Reverend," he said, "my drinking has gotten so bad, I want to take the pledge. I'm ready—I'll never drink again as long as I live!"

"Well," the minister said, "you're certainly welcome to come in, but I don't think I have an actual copy of the pledge."

"Thas okay, pastor," Jim Bob slurred, "I know it by heart."

Wisdom _"Jesus replied: 'Love the Lord your God with all your heart and with all your soul and with all your mind. This is the first and greatest commandment. And the second is like it: Love your neighbor as yourself. All the Law and the Prophets hang on these two commandments.'"_
— _Matthew 22:37-40 (NIV)_

This is me ...
I love God with all my heart, soul and mind. I love my neighbors as myself.

Journal

Date _____

Chuckle "I live in a dysfunctional home and it's really difficult," admitted a newcomer at a meeting, "especially since I live alone."

Wisdom *"And God spoke all these words: 'I am the Lord your God, who brought you out of Egypt, out of the land of slavery. You shall have no other God besides me.'"*

— Exodus 20:1-3 (NIV)

This is me ...
God set me free. He lead me out of slavery and into a place of serene peace.

Journal

Date _____

Chuckle You might be an alcoholic if:
• The booze that you're drinking reminds you of the taste of a fine aftershave.
• You awaken in your water bed all warm and comfy when you remember you don't have a water bed.
• When a cop pulls you over and you offer him a beer."

Wisdom _"Love isn't love until you give it away."_

— _Roger Hammerstein_

This is me ...
I choose the values my Father God has placed within my heart and live my life accordingly.

Journal

Chuckle A hundred years ago it was easier to get home while drunk, because your horse was sober.

Wisdom *"And we know that in all things God works for the good of those who love him, who have been called according to his purpose."*
— Romans 8:28 (NIV)

This is me ...
I am, as ever, in bewildered awe of all that my loving Father God has done to ransom and rescue me.

Journal

Date _____

Chuckle What is the difference between an al-anon and an alcoholic? An al-anon will steal money from you and then admit it and apologize. An alcoholic will steal money from you and then help you look for it.

Wisdom _"Jesus said, 'If you hold to my teaching, you are really my disciples. Then you will know the truth, and the truth will set you free.'"_
— _John 8:31-32 (NIV)_

This is me ...
The healing presence of God has set me free in every way.

Journal

Date _____

Chuckle A dude with a serious case of the munchies went into a pizza parlor and ordered an extra large pizza to go. The girl at the counter asked, "Would you like your pizza cut into 8 or 12 pieces?"

"Whoa, maaan," said the stoner, "I can't eat that many pieces—cut it into six."

Wisdom *"If I had eight hours to chop down a tree, I'd spend six sharpening my axe."*

— *Abraham Lincoln*

This is me ...
I bloom where I'm planted.

Journal

Date _____

Chuckle A couple was sitting in a romantic corner of a restaurant enjoying cocktails. Suddenly, the waiter ran up to the table.

"Miss," the waiter exclaimed, "your husband just slid under the table!"

"No," the woman replied, "my husband just walked in the door."

Wisdom *"Be merciful to those who doubt; snatch others from the fire and save them; to others show mercy, mixed with fear—hating even the clothing stained by corrupted flesh. To him who is able to keep you from falling and to present you before his glorious presence without fault and with great joy—to the only God our Savior be glory, majesty, power and authority, through Jesus Christ our Lord, before all ages, now and forevermore! Amen."*

— Jude 1:22-24 (NIV)

This is me ...
I have the hope and the gift of life beyond this world. My great God has granted me this freely through faith in His bountiful provision. My God is all powerful and always acts with love. I will seek to accept His gift and fulfill His desire for me to be with Him forever.

Journal

Date _____

Chuckle "People who stay in the middle of the road get run over."

— _Aneurin Bevan_

Wisdom _"Therefore let him who thinks he stands take heed that he does not fall. No temptation has overtaken you but such as is common to man; and God is faithful, who will not allow you to be tempted beyond what you are able, but with the temptation will provide the way of escape also, so that you will be able to endure it."_

— _1 Corinthians 10:12-13 (NASB)_

This is me ...
As a corn plant is perfect in each stage of its growth process—I am perfect in each stage of my spiritual growth process.

Journal

Date _____

Chuckle "The god most people believe in couldn't get into heaven."
— *William Roylance*

Wisdom *"God grant me the serenity to accept the things I cannot change, the courage to change the things I can, and the wisdom to know the difference. Living one day at a time, accepting hardship as a pathway to peace, taking as Jesus did, this sinful world as it is, not as I would have it. Trusting that You will make all things right if I surrender to Your will; so that I may be reasonably happy in this life, and supremely happy with You forever in the next."*
— *The Serenity Prayer, unabridged*

This is me ...
I am in eternity now.

Journal

Date _____

Chuckle A tired old alky found a bottle on the beach, opened it and set free a genie, who said, "Thank you! I've been a prisoner in there for fifty years!"

"I know just how you feel," sighed the drunk."

Wisdom *"Since, then, you have been raised with Christ, set your hearts on things above, where Christ is seated at the right hand of God. Set your minds on things above, not on earthly things. For you died, and your life is now hidden with Christ in God. When Christ, who is your life, appears, then you also will appear with him in glory."*
— *Colossians 3:1-4 (NIV)*

This is me ...
I clothe myself with peace, joy, compassion, kindness, humility, gentleness, faithfulness, patience and love.

Journal

Date _____

Chuckle Jim and Bob were riding a New York City subway when a man approached them, asking for spare change. Jim refused.

Bob, on the other hand, whipped out his wallet, pulled out a ten dollar bill, and handed it to the bum.

Jim was outraged. "What did you do that for?" He shouted. "Don't you know he's only going to use the money for drugs or booze?"

"Hellooo, and we weren't?" Bob replied.

Wisdom *Live and let live.*

— Unknown

This is me ...
One of the greateist joys I will ever know is doing what I should do because I want to.

Journal

Date _____

Chuckle I told my sponsor, "Hey dude, you don't understand, I'm like a rebel without a cause, maaan."

"No," he replied, "you're like a rebel without a clue."

Wisdom _"For I know the thoughts that I think toward you, says the LORD, thoughts of peace and not of evil, to give you a future and a hope."_
— Jeremiah 29:11 (NLT)

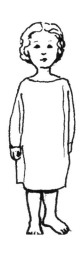

This is me ...
I treat everyone as they are, a dignified, beautiful child of God.

Journal

Date _____

Chuckle "I drink to make other
people interesting."

— George Jean Nathan

Wisdom "I no longer want the
cheese, I just want out of the trap."

— Spanish proverb

This is me ...
I have discovered the steps out of the
trap.

Journal

Date _____

Chuckle Sounds of wild partying are coming from inside a bar. Two highway patrolmen are watching the place waiting for someone to drive away so they can arrest them for drunk driving.

At 1:50 AM, Jim Bob comes staggering out the front door, stumbles to his car, gets in, starts it up, leans against the steering wheel and starts playing with the radio. The cops wait patiently to catch him driving as everyone else in the bar comes out and drives off.

As soon as everyone is out of sight Jim Bob drives away and the police make their move.

They pull him over and ask him. "Just how much have you had to drink?"

"Not a drop," grins Jim Bob. "I'm the designated decoy."

Wisdom _"I like the dreams of the future better than the history of the past."_

— _Thomas Jefferson_

This is me ...
I do not live in the past, I do not future trip. I enjoy each moment.

Journal

Date _____

Chuckle A tweaker at a laundromat keeps dropping coins into the slots of the vending machines and piling the food on nearby tables. On his fourth trip for change, the cashier asks him, "Just what are you doing?"
"Doing…?" The tweaker replies, "I'm winning, maaaan!"

Wisdom _"No man has a good enough memory to make a successful liar."_
— Jerry Moore

This is me …
Faith fills all voids. God consumes my every waking thought.

Journal

Date _____

Chuckle The young al-anon said to her newly sober alcoholic husband, I liked you better when you were drinking!"

"I know how you feel," replied the newcomer. "When I was drinking I liked you better, too."

Wisdom *"The only gift is a portion of thyself."*

— *Ralph Waldo Emerson*

This is me ...
I learn best how to give from my Father God who freely gives me everything for the enjoyment I obtain in sharing it with others.
Thank you Father.

Journal

Date _____

Chuckle Once upon a time there was a woman who took drugs just to steady her nerves. The other night she got so steady, she couldn't move.

Wisdom _"Wives, be subject to your husbands, as is fitting in the Lord. Husbands, love your wives and do not be embittered against them._

Children, be obedient to your parents in all things, for this is well-pleasing to the Lord.

Fathers, do not exasperate your children, so that they will not lose heart.

Slaves, in all things obey those who are your masters on earth, not with external service, as those who merely please men, but with sincerity of heart, fearing the Lord."
— _Colossians 3:18-22 (NASB)_

This is me ...
Gratitude is my favorite attitude.

Journal

Date _____

Chuckle A stock broker confronted a panhandler outside of his office, demanding to know, "Is this the only way you can make a living?"

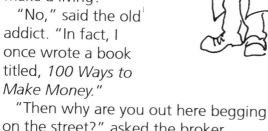

"No," said the old addict. "In fact, I once wrote a book titled, _100 Ways to Make Money._"

"Then why are you out here begging on the street?" asked the broker.

"Well," shrugged the shaky old druggy, "this was one of them."

Wisdom _"Find a way, or make one."_
— _Lucius Seneca_

This is me ...
Time is not an enemy to be beat, it is a part of the rhythm of my life. Each day, I pause to enjoy sweet moments of timeless serenity.

Journal

Date _____

Chuckle Jim Bob stood before the judge on charges of holding up a liquor store and taking 20 bottles of whiskey, while leaving the cash register untouched.

The judge asked, "Why didn't you take the money?"

Jim Bob responded, "I'd just blow it on booze."

Wisdom *"'It is the Spirit who gives life; the flesh profits nothing; the words that I have spoken to you are spirit and are life. But there are some of you who do not believe.' For Jesus knew from the beginning who they were who did not believe, and who it was that would betray Him. And He was saying, 'For this reason I have said to you, that no one can come to Me unless it has been granted him from the Father.'"*

— *John 6:63-65 (NASB)*

This is me ...
I am continually learning to let God more fully into my heart.

_____

_____

_____

_____

_____

_____

_____

_____

_____

_____

Journal

Date _____

Chuckle My five-year-old son had heard me say, "I need a meeting" so often that one day, when I picked him up and asked what he wanted to do, he said, "Dad, I really need a cartoon."

Wisdom *"How can a young man keep his way pure?*
By living according to your word.
I seek you with all my heart;
do not let me stray from your commands.
I have hidden your word in my heart that I might not sin against you.
Praise be to you, O LORD;
teach me your decrees.
With my lips I recount all the laws that come from your mouth.
I rejoice in following your statutes as one rejoices in great riches.
I meditate on your precepts and consider your ways.
I delight in your decrees;
I will not neglect your word."
— *Psalms 119:9-16 (NIV)*

This is me ...
I keep my ways pure by living according to God's word.
I seek Him with all my heart and do not stray from His will.
I rejoice in following Him.
I delight in knowing His desires for me each day.

Journal

Date _____

Chuckle A newcomer approached her sponsor and asked, "What do I do when I am done with all Twelve Steps?"

The sponsor replied, "Lie very, very still—because you're dead"

Wisdom _"The reward of humility and the fear of the Lord, are riches, honor and life."_

— _Proverbs 22:4 (NASB)_

This is me ...
"Two men look out through the bars. One sees the mud, the other the stars." I see the stars.

— _F. Longbridge_

Journal

Date _____

Chuckle: Notice on an NA bulletin Board: "Lost dog:
• Missing a paw
• Toothless
• Left ear chewed in half
• Answers to name of 'Lucky'."

Wisdom _"Good people are good because they've come to wisdom through failure."_

— _William Saroyan_

This is me ...
I learn from the mistakes of others as well as my own.

Journal

Date _____

Chuckle A cop pulls Jim Bob over and says, "You were doing fifty miles per hour in a thirty-mile-an-hour zone." Jim Bob replies, "I most certainly was not!"

"Yes, you were," the officer insists.

"No, I wasn't," repeats Jim Bob.

At this point his wife, Helen, speaks up. "Don't waste your time officer, It is useless to argue with him when he's drunk."

Wisdom _"All things have been committed to me by my Father. No one knows the Son except the Father, and no one knows the Father except the Son and those to whom the Son chooses to reveal him._

"Come to me, all you who are weary and burdened, and I will give you rest. Take my yoke upon you and learn from me, for I am gentle and humble in heart, and you will find rest for your souls. For my yoke is easy and my burden is light."

— _Matthew 11:27-30 (NIV)_

This is me ...
I have found a safe place to rest—my Father God's presence.

Journal

Date _____

Chuckle How do you make God laugh?—Tell Him your plans.

Wisdom _"Do not be deceived, God is not be mocked; for whatever a man sows this he will also reap. The one who sows to his own flesh will from the flesh reap corruption, but the one who sows to the Spirit will from the Spirit reap eternal life. Let us not lose heart in doing good, for in due time we will reap if we do not grow weary. So then, while we have opportunity, let us do good to all people, and especially to those who are of the household of the faith."_

— Galatians 6:7-10 (NASB)

This is me ...
The eyes of my heart remain fixed on God.

Journal

Date _____

Chuckle A drunk was arrested and thrown in jail. Two days later she came to and asked the jailer on duty, "What am I here for?"

The officer said "For drinking."

The drunk exclaimed, "That's great! When do we start?"

Wisdom _"Whoever loves discipline loves knowledge, but he who hates correction is stupid."_

— _Proverbs 12:1. NIV_

This is me ...
I am guided by God to make the right decisions.

Journal

Date _____

Chuckle Jim and Bob were sitting at the bar arguing over whose dog was the smartest. Jim said, "My dog sits on the porch every morning and waits for the paper and then brings it to me."

Bob responded, "I know, my dog told me."

Wisdom _"Therefore, since we have been justified through faith, we have peace with God through our Lord Jesus Christ, through whom we have gained access by faith into this grace in which we now stand. And we rejoice in the hope of the glory of God. Not only so, but we also rejoice in our sufferings, because we know that suffering produces perseverance; perseverance, character; and character, hope. And hope does not disappoint us, because God has poured out his love into our hearts by the Holy Spirit, whom he has given us._

You see, at just the right time, when we were still powerless, Christ died for the ungodly. Very rarely will anyone die for a righteous man, though for a good man someone might possibly dare to die. But God demonstrates his own love for us in this: While we were still sinners, Christ died for us."

— _Romans 5:1-8 (NIV)_

This is me ...
I am blind to the faults of others.

Journal

Date _____

Chuckle That light at the end of the tunnel may be you.

Wisdom _"Sow a thought and reap an act; sow an act and reap a habit; sow a habit and reap a character; sow a character and reap a destiny."_

— Ralph Waldo Emerson

This is me ...
Because my thoughts will become my destiny, I guard them with extreme diligence.

Journal

Date _____

Chuckle Dear Lord, so far today I've been doing great. I haven't gossiped, I haven't been angry; I haven't been prideful, lustful, selfish, or overindulgent. But in a few minutes, Lord, I'm going to get out of bed, and from then on, I'm probably going to need a lot of help.

Wisdom _"Be anxious for nothing, but in everything by prayer and supplication with thanksgiving let your requests be made known to God. And the peace of God, which surpasses all comprehension, will guard your hearts and your minds in Christ Jesus._

Finally, brethren, whatever is true, whatever is honorable, whatever is right, whatever is pure, whatever is lovely, whatever is of good repute, if there is any excellence and if anything worthy of praise, dwell on these things.

The things you have learned and received and heard and seen in me, practice these things, and the God of peace will be with you."
— _Philippians 4:6-9 (NASB)_

This is me ...
I am perfectly peaceful as I rest quietly in His presence.

Journal

Date _____

Chuckle Jim Bob staggered down an alley when he was jumped by five guys. After a hard struggle, the thugs got him down and searched his pockets; however, all they found was 25 cents.

"Man," said one of the robbers, "you put up quite a fight for 25 cents!"

"Is that all you wanted?" Jim Bob laughed. "I thought that you were after the five hundred bucks that I have hidden in my shoe!"

Wisdom _"You have heard that it was said, 'Eye for eye, and tooth for tooth.' But I tell you, Do not resist an evil person. If someone strikes you on the right cheek, turn to him the other also. And if someone wants to sue you and take your tunic, let him have your cloak as well."_

— Matthew 5:38-40 (NIV)

This is me ...
I am humble, considerate and submissive to God. I am full of mercy and good fruit, impartial, sincere and loving.

Journal

Chuckle Jim and Bob were sitting in a bar knocking back a few drinks and talking about their wives. Jim complained, "My wife has such good hearing that no matter how quietly I try to sneak into the house, she wakes up and bugs me about my drinking."

"Not mine," said Bob. "She's such a sound sleeper that when I come home I usually run over the garbage can, rattle and bang the doors, kick the cat, turn on all the lights on, fall down the stairs backwards while cussing loudly, drop my shoes on the floor, jump into bed and holler, 'Hey, Darlin', how about some of that sweet lovin?' She just sleeps like a baby through it all!"

Wisdom *"Offer hospitality to one another without grumbling. Each of you should use whatever gifts you have received to serve others, as faithful stewards of God's grace in its various forms. If you speak, you should do so as one who speaks the very words of God. If you serve, you should do it with the strength God provides, so that in all things God may be praised through Jesus Christ. To him be the glory and the power for ever and ever. Amen."*

— *1 Peter 4:9-11 (TNIV)*

This is me ...
I keep what I have by continually giving it away.

Journal

Date _____

Chuckle My alcoholic mind would have killed my alcoholic body a long time ago except it needed it for transportation.

Wisdom *"'Do not let your hearts be troubled; believe in God, believe also in Me. In My Father's house are many dwelling places; if it were not so, I would have told you; for I go to prepare a place for you. If I go and prepare a place for you, I will come again and receive you to Myself, that where I am, there you may be also. And you know the way where I am going.'"*

Thomas said to Him, 'Lord, we do not know where You are going, how do we know the way?'

Jesus said to him, 'I am the way, and the truth, and the life; no one comes to the Father but through Me.'"

— John 14:1-6 (NASB)

This is me ...
I can live forever because of what God has done for me.

Journal

Date _____

Chuckle Any drunk can get into AA, but to get into Al-Anon, you have to know somebody.

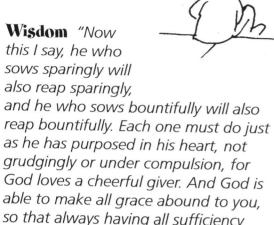

Wisdom _"Now this I say, he who sows sparingly will also reap sparingly, and he who sows bountifully will also reap bountifully. Each one must do just as he has purposed in his heart, not grudgingly or under compulsion, for God loves a cheerful giver. And God is able to make all grace abound to you, so that always having all sufficiency in everything, you may have an abundance for every good deed..."_

— _2 Corinthians 9:6-8 (NASB)_

This is me ...
As I give I receive.

Journal

Date _____

Chuckle "Will work for food" is a message on signs that many panhandlers use today to get handouts, but one honest fellow held a sign that stated: "Why lie? I need a drink."

Wisdom *"Do not love the world nor the things in the world. If anyone loves the world, the love of the Father is not in him. For all that is in the world, the lust of the flesh and the lust of the eyes and the boastful pride of life, is not from the Father, but is from the world. The world is passing away, and also its lusts; but the one who does the will of God lives forever."*
— 1 John 2:15-17 (NASB)

This is me ...
I humbly rely on prayer as a means of obtaining divine assistance to transform my character defects into assets for helping others.

Journal

Date _____

Chuckle An old timer was explaining to a new comer. "You can get off the elevator that takes you to the bottom floor of the drug addict ride any time you want. But in order to get back to the top, you have to take the Steps."

Wisdom _"Love is the forgetting of oneself in the service of another."_

— R. Ainsley Barnwell

This is me ...
The grace of God does for me what I could never do for myself.

Journal

Date _____

Chuckle After a long night of drinkin' and druggin', Jim and Bob became close friends and agreed to meet again in five years in the same bar, at the same time.

Five years later Jim walked in the door and sure enough, there was Bob, sitting at the bar.

Jim hugged his old friend and cried, "The night we left, I didn't think I'd really see you here again!"

Bob looked up from his glass and said, "Who left?"

Wisdom _"A fool finds pleasure in evil conduct, but a man of understanding delights in wisdom."_

— _Proverbs 10:23 (NIV)_

This is me ...
I develop only beneficial habits.

Journal

Date _____

Chuckle After many years of sobriety, an old timer was sharing at a meeting that he was baby sitting his infant granddaughter. As he watched her he bent over and whispered in her ear, "You know, darlin', I used to be just like you: a bottle in my mouth and a mess in my pants."

Wisdom *"The more that I appreciate and love the mysterious being that I am, the less I long to be someone else."*

— *Unknown*

This is me ...
I can look the world in the eye.

Journal

Date _____

Chuckle Alcohol is truly the world's greatest solvent: drink enough of it and it'll dissolve your marriage, your family, your property, your job, your body— and anything else with which it comes in contact.

Wisdom *"You whom I have taken from the ends of the earth, and called from its remotest parts and said to you, 'You are My servant, I have chosen you and not rejected you. Do not fear, for I am with you; do not anxiously look about you, for I am your God. I will strengthen you, surely I will help you, surely I will uphold you with My righteous right hand.'"*

— Isaiah 41:9-10 (NASB)

This is me ...
I seek humility as something I really desire rather than as something I must do.
When I am humble, I am at peace.

Journal

Date _____

Chuckle Jim and Bob were trying to decide which business venture to embark upon: "You know Jim, I think we should buy a bar," said Bob.

  "Why a bar?" replied Jim.

  "Just think—a bar's the only business where if you throw a customer out the front door, he'll just pick himself up off the street and fight to get back in!"

Wisdom _"Children have never been very good at listening to their elders, but they have never failed to imitate them."_

— James Baldwin

This is me ...
I love to obey my heavenly Father because I know He only wants what is best for me.

Journal

Date _____

Chuckle Most of us don't change because we see the light; but because we feel the heat.

Wisdom *"Be not afraid of greatness; some are born great, some achieve greatness, and some have greatness thrust upon them."*

— *Shakespeare*

This is me ...
I don't need the handwriting on the wall to know when I am doing something wrong. God's still small voice within me is my inner guide. He directs me through the maze of rationalization and justification.

Journal

Date _____

Chuckle Politically-correct statements: Not "drug addicts," but "chemically challenged."

   It is not a "beer gut," it is an "energy storage unit."

Wisdom *"You will seek me and find me when you seek me with all your heart."*

— *Jeremiah 29:13 (NASB)*

This is me ...
I am here to love and serve.

Journal

Date _____

Chuckle An old hippie with a large parrot on his shoulder dropped into a tavern to get a drink. "My good Lord!" exclaimed the bartender, "Where in heaven's name did you find that?" "Just stop at any bar around here and you'll find a bunch of them," replied the parrot.

Wisdom _"Who of us is mature enough for offspring before the offspring themselves arrive? The value of marriage is not that adults produce children but that children produce adults."_

— _Peter De Vries_

This is me ...
In earnestly working the steps, I have developed an awareness and understanding of my thought and action patterns. This was necessary to help prevent a relapse into old behavior. I now practice the principles of the Twelve Steps in all my affairs. Doing this makes new positive patterns develop and pushes out the old negative ones. I love how this method works. It certainly beats trying to fight my defects of character.

Journal

Date _____

Chuckle New alcohol warning label: Warning: The consumption of alcohol may cause pregnancy.

Wisdom _"Love must be learned, and learned again and again; there is no end to it. Hate needs no instruction, but only waits to be provoked."_
— _Katherine Anne Porter_

This is me ...
I do not expect others or myself to be perfect before we are deserving of love and acceptance.

Journal

Date _____

Chuckle Call before you take a drink and I will help you stay sober. Call after you take a drink and you will help me stay sober.

Wisdom _I was regretting the past and fearing the future._
Suddenly my Lord was speaking:
"My name is I am"
He paused.
I waited. He continued,
"When you live in the past with its mistakes and regrets, it is hard. I am not there. My name is not I WAS.
When you live in the future, with its problems and fears, it is hard. I am not there. My name is not I WILL BE.
When you live in this moment it is not hard. I am here. My name I AM."
— Helen Mallicoat

This is me ...
"When I grow up I want to be like a little child."
— Joseph Heller

Journal

Date _____

Chuckle Jim and Bob were out late one rainy night. As they arrived back at the car Jim discovered that he had lost his keys. He found a coat hanger in a dumpster and was busy trying to open the door while Bob just staggered around the car acting disgusted. "Finally," Bob said, "You had better hurry up and get the door open man. It's raining hard and your top is down, man."

Wisdom *"Forgiving is not forgetting, it's letting go of the hurt."*

— *Mary McLeod Bethune*

This is me ...
Honesty is my constant aim. I know that this takes practice, so I practice honesty like my life depended upon it, because it does.

Journal

Date _____

Chuckle What's the difference between a good friend and a true friend? A good friend will come bail you out of jail. A true friend will be sitting in the cell right next to you.

Wisdom *"Therefore, since we have a great high priest who has passed through the heavens, Jesus the Son of God, let us hold fast our confession. For we do not have a high priest who cannot sympathize with our weaknesses, but One who has been tempted in all things as we are, yet without sin.*

Therefore let us draw near with confidence to the throne of grace, so that we may receive mercy and find grace to help in time of need."
— *Hebrews 4:14-16 (NASB)*

This is me ...
As I rise above my addictions I see everything in a new and wonderful light. God is light.

Journal

Date _____

Chuckle Yet another new alcohol warning label: Warning: The consumption of alcohol may cause you to believe that people are laughing with you.

Wisdom _"The mass of men lead lives of quiet desperation."_

— _Henry David Thoreau_

This is me ...
I dwell in uninterrupted steadfastness because I know who my God is.

Journal

Date _____

Chuckle I took a sip out of the bottle, and then the bottle took a gulp out of me.

Wisdom _"As the Father has loved me, so have I loved you. Now remain in my love. If you keep my commands, you will remain in my love, just as I have kept my Father's commands and remain in his love. I have told you this so that my joy may be in you and that your joy may be complete. My command is this: Love each other as I have loved you. Greater love has no one than this: to lay down one's life for one's friends."_

— John 15:9-13 (NIV)

This is me ...
I will lay down my life for my friends. This is what God has done for me. In doing this I will find His joy—complete joy.

Chuckle Alcoholics are like tea bags. They won't work unless they are in hot water.

Wisdom *"This is eternal life, that they may know You, the only true God, and Jesus Christ, whom you have sent."*
— *John 17:3 (NASB)*

This is me ...
My greatest desire is to know Him.

Journal

Date _____

Chuckle Okay, just one more new alcohol warning label: _Warning_: The consumption of alcohol may cause you to believe that you are a world class fighter about the same time that you are losing your muscle coordination.

Wisdom _"Honesty is the first chapter in the book of wisdom."_

— _Thomas Jefferson_

This is me ...
I am honest.

Journal

Date _____

Chuckle An Irishman walks out of a bar?

Wisdom *"Truly I say to you, whoever says to his mountain, 'Be taken up and cast into the sea,' and does not doubt in his heart, but believes that what he says is going to happen, it will be granted him.*
Therefore I say to you, all things for which you pray and ask, believe that you have received them, and they will be granted you."
— *Mark 11:23-24 (NASB)*

This is me ...
I believe.

Journal

Date _____

Chuckle An old, completely baked stoner was stumbling down the street, dragging an armchair behind him. A policeman stopped him and asked, "Hey, man, what are you doing dragging that chair?" The stoner looked him in the eye and said, "Did you ever try to push one?"

Wisdom _"Beloved, let us love one another, for love is from God; and everyone who loves is born of God and knows God. The one who does not love does not know God, for God is love."_

— _1 John 4:7-8 (NASB)_

This is me ...
"Love is patient, love is kind. It does not envy, it does not boast, it is not proud, it is not rude. It is not self-seeking, it is not easily angered, it keeps no record of wrongs. Love does not delight in evil but rejoices with the truth. It always protects, always trusts, always hopes, always perseveres. Love never fails." I am love.

— _1 Corinthians 13:4-8 (NIV)_

Journal

Date _____

Chuckle Helen and Jim Bob went to the dentist. Helen approached the dentist and said, "I want a tooth pulled and I don't want you to use any pain killers because I am in a hurry."

"You are a very brave women," the dentist told Helen, "which tooth do you want pulled."

She turned to Jim Bob and said, "Okay, idiot, show him your bad tooth."

Wisdom _"Earth is crammed with heaven. And every common bush is afire with God."_

— _Elizabeth Barrett Browning_

This is me ...
The grace of God has set me on fire.

Journal

Date _____

Chuckle Okay, just one more alcohol warning label: Warning: The consumption of alcohol may cause you to believe that you can carry on an enchanting conversation with an attractive member of the opposite sex.

Wisdom *"'Our Father who is in heaven, Hallowed be your name, your kingdom come, your will be done, on earth as it is in heaven.*

Give us this day our daily bread.

And forgive our debts, as we also have forgiven our debtors.

And do not lead us into temptation, but deliver us from evil.

(For Yours is the kingdom and the power and the glory forever. Amen)

For if you forgive others for their transgressions, your heavenly Father will also forgive you. But if you do not forgive others, then your Father will not forgive your transgressions.'"

— *Matthew 6:9-15 (NASB)*

This is me ...
I can accept the increased knowledge and awareness that recovery brings—without punishing myself for what I didn't know before I arrived.

Journal

Chuckle I caught my wife flirting."
"Nice, that's how I caught mine, too."

Wisdom *"Therefore, there is now no condemnation for those who are in Christ Jesus. For the law of the Spirit of life has set me free from the law of sin and death."*

— *Romans 8:1,2 (NIV)*

This is me ...
I no longer feel guilty about the past. The steps set me free. I will continue to work them as I allow God to remove the defects that block me from the sunlight of His Spirit.

Journal

Date _____

Chuckle Jim and Bob had a drunken argument which eventually landed them in court. Near the end of the trial, just before the judge was to decide the case, Jim asked his lawyer, "Do you think that I should send the judge a box of cigars? It might help him lean in our favor."

"Oh, absolutely not!" replied the lawyer. "This judge is really nasty when it comes to bribery. I am sure that if you sent him a gift, he would rule against you—and may even hold you in contempt of court!"

The next day the judge delivered his decision in favor of Jim. As they were leaving the court room, Jim turned to his lawyer and said, "Thanks for the tip about the cigars."

"You're welcome," answered the lawyer, "I'm happy that you didn't send them."

"I did send them," said Jim, "but I put Bob's business card in the box."

Wisdom _"I am not bound to win, but I am bound to be true. I am not bound to succeed, but I am bound to live up to the light I have."_

— _Abraham Lincoln_

This is me ...
I will not exchange the future as a compensation for the present. Life exists only here and now. I will be here now.

Journal

Date _____

Chuckle Sign in a bar: This was a single door when you came in. If it is a double door now; please aim for the middle.

Wisdom _"Do not judge so that you will not be judged. For in the way you judge, you will be judged; and by your standard of measure, it will be measured to you."_

— _Matthew 7:1-2 (NASB)_

This is me ...
I only need to take one person's inventory—my own.

Journal

Date _____

Chuckle After a week-long trial, Jim Bob suddenly changed his plea to guilty. The angry judge screamed, "You idiot! This case has taken up a week of my time, the prosecutor's time, the legal aid office's time, and the jury's time—why are you confessing now?"

"Well, your Honor," stammered Jim Bob, "until I saw the evidence, I thought I was innocent!"

Wisdom *"Behind an able person there are always other able people."*
— Chinese proverb

This is me ...
I am grateful for all the people who make up the mosaic of my life.

Journal

Date _____

Chuckle Jim Bob finally began to believe that he had a drinking problem when he discovered that he could only afford a $100 car because he had to fork over $10,000 for the insurance to drive it."

Wisdom *"'So I say to you: Ask and it will be given to you; seek and you will find; knock and the door will be opened to you. For everyone who asks receives; those who seek find; and to those who knock, the door will be opened.'"*

— Luke 11:9-10 (TNIV)

This is me ...
I truly enjoy the study of God's word. It keeps me close to Him. That is where home is. That is where my heart is.

Journal

Date _____

Chuckle After many years of relapsing, her sponsor finally told her what the word SLIP stood for: Sobriety Losing Its Priority.

Wisdom _"A man should never be ashamed to own that he has been in the wrong, which is but saying, in other words, that he is wiser today than he was yesterday."_

— _Alexander Pope_

This is me ...
When I sleep my sub-conscious mind finds solutions to challenges and often enlightens me with the best alternatives. It is a good thing to— "Sleep on it."

Journal

Date _____

Chuckle I was trying to hold on to some old ideas when my sponsor told me to "let go or be dragged."

Wisdom *"You know what has happened throughout the province of Judea, beginning in Galilee after the baptism that John preached—how God anointed Jesus of Nazareth with the Holy Spirit and power, and how he went around doing good and healing all who were under the power of the devil, because God was with him.*
We are witnesses of everything he did in the country of the Jews and in Jerusalem. They killed him by hanging him on a cross, but God raised him from the dead on the third day and caused him to be seen.
He was not seen by all the people, but by witnesses whom God had already chosen—by us who ate and drank with him after he rose from the dead. He commanded us to preach to the people and to testify that he is the one whom God appointed as judge of the living and the dead."

— *Acts 10:37-42 (NIV)*

This is me ...
I am prepared for the day that Jesus will return and take me home.
I have faith in His freely granted gift of eternal life.

Journal

Date _____

Chuckle Addicts are like tug boats: they are the loudest when they're in the fog.

Wisdom *"Then he said to them, 'Beware, and be on your guard against every form of greed; for not even when one has an abundance does his life consist of his possessions.'"*
— *Luke 12:15 (NASB)*

This is me ...
The best things in life aren't things. Things will never satisfy the deep longings of my heart. It is being useful to God and his children that bring true joy.

Journal

Date _____

Chuckle There was an overly ambitious lady executive who had a drinking problem. At the wake of her recently deceased boss, she spotted the owner  of the company. After downing 10 or 12 martinis, she got brave and decided to boldly ask him if she might now take her supervisor's place. The owner replied, "If it's okay with the undertaker, it is fine with me."

Wisdom _"In the beginner's mind there are many possibilities, but in the expert's there are few."_

— _Shunyu Suzuki_

This is me ...
My sponser often repeats a reliable philosophy to me - "Keep It Simple Sweetheart."

Journal

Date _____

Chuckle Jim Bob was sitting on a park bench when a young woman walked up to him with a notebook in her hand and said, "Sir, I am working on a study on how to live a long life, and since you look rather elderly, could you give me your insights on how to do that?"

"You bet," said Jim Bob. "I smoke three packs of cigarettes a day, and I drink a gallon of booze every day before I attempt to eat something. When I can finally eat, I eat only fatty foods and I never exercise."

"That is amazing," replied the student. "Just how old are you?"

Jim Bob gave her a toothless smile and replied, "I am twenty-eight."

Wisdom *"Take care, brethren, that there not be in any one of you an evil, unbelieving heart that falls away from the living God. But encourage one another day after day, as long as it is still called 'Today,' so that none of you will be hardened by the deceitfulness of sin."*

— Hebrews 3:12,13 (NASB)

This is me ...
I no longer need to be right. I only need to love and serve.

Journal

Date _____

Chuckle A normal drinker finds a fly in his beer and asks the bartender to pour him a fresh drink. A heavy drinker finds a fly in his beer, pulls it out by the wings, and continues drinking. An alcoholic finds a fly in his beer and yells, "Spit it out! Spit it out!"

Wisdom *"Don't be deceived, my dear brothers and sisters. Every good and perfect gift is from above, coming down from the Father of the heavenly lights, who does not change like shifting shadows. He chose to give us birth through the word of truth, that we might be a kind of first-fruits of all he created. My dear brothers and sisters, take note of this: Everyone should be quick to listen, slow to speak and slow to become angry, because human anger does not produce the righteousness that God desires."*

— James 1:16-20 (NIV)

This is me ...
I am not self-deceived. I see who I am—a joint heirs with Jesus. I will conduct my life like royalty. For my brother is King of kings and Lord of lords.

Journal

Date _____

Chuckle A stoner called the fire department and said, "I think my house is on fire, maaan. Will you come over and help me?"

"Yes, sir," the dispatcher responded. "How do we get there?"

"Hey, maaan," replied the stoner. "Don't you still use those big red trucks, maaan?"

Wisdom _"If you can't get rid of the family skeleton, you may as well make it dance."_

— George Bernard Shaw

This is me ...
I am free of the guilt and remorse that kept me bound in the cycle of addiction.

Journal

Date _____

Chuckle Jim Bob was in detox—he started having hallucinations about the Seven Deadly Dwarfs: Sleazy, Porky, Whiney, Lazy, Meany, Greedy and Grumpy.

Wisdom *"In you, O Lord, I have taken refuge; let me never be ashamed; In Your righteousness deliver me. Incline your ear to me, rescue me quickly; be to me a rock of strength, a stronghold to save me.*

For You are my rock and my fortress; for Your name's sake You will lead me and guide me. You will pull me out of the net which they have secretly laid for me, for You are my strength.

Into Your hand I commit my spirit; You have ransomed me, O Lord, God of truth."

— *Psalm 31:1-5 (NASB)*

This is me ...
I am grateful for all that God freely grants me, especially the ease and comfort that comes from knowing— He is running the show—not me.

Journal

Date _____

Chuckle Two newcomers, Jim and Bob, were talking about the treatment centers that they had gone to.

Jim asked Bob, "Hey, maaan, did you go to Betty Ford?"

"No," replied Bob. "I went to Helen Back!"

Wisdom _"Consider it pure joy, my brothers and sisters, whenever you face trials of many kinds, because you know that the testing of your faith produces perseverance. Let perseverance finish its work so that you may be mature and complete, not lacking anything. If any of you lacks wisdom, you should ask God, who gives generously to all without finding fault, and it will be given to you."_

— James 1:2-5 (NIV)

This is me ...
I may not be comfortable in all life situations, but I can always be joyful. I will persevere and watch for the lessons, for they are always there in the midst of the trials.

Journal

Date _____

Chuckle   When asked where he lived, Jim Bob replied, "The 23rd Precinct."

Wisdom   *"Fools mock at sin, but among the upright there is good will."*
— *Proverbs 14:9 (NASB)*

This is me ...
I have better relationships with others when I am true to myself.

Journal

Date _____

Chuckle After listening to a newcomer in the program his sponsor told him,

"I think you're going to go far in this Fellowship," the sponsor reported.

"Excellent," the newcomer replied. "Why do you think that, man?"

"Because you have such a long way to go," the sponsor answered.

Wisdom _"See what great love the Father has lavished on us, that we should be called children of God! And that is what we are! The reason the world does not know us is that it did not know him. Dear friends, now we are children of God, and what we will be has not yet been made known. But we know that when Christ appears, we shall be like him, for we shall see him as he is. All who have this hope in him purify themselves, just as he is pure."_
— _1 John 3:1-3 (NIV)_

This is me ...
As I treat others well, I automatically treat myself well. What goes around comes around.

Journal

Date _____

Chuckle Jim Bob took his drunken dog to the vet: "Doc, I think my dog is dead."

The vet set his dog on the table, brought in a cat and had the cat walk up and down on top of the dog.

"Yes, Jim Bob, your dog is dead. That will be $500."

"$500!" exclaims Jim Bob, "for what?"

"It's $50 for the office call," the vet replied, "and $450 for the Cat Scan."

Wisdom *"The only time you can't afford to fail is the last time you try."*
— *Charles Kettering*

This is me ...
I never perform at a lower level than I am able just because others cannot handle my extraordinary success.

Journal

Date _____

Chuckle On New Year's Eve the bartender was nearly crushed to death when Jim Bob yelled out at the stroke of midnight, "It's time! Now everybody kiss the person that makes your life worth living.

Wisdom *"Forgiveness creates gravity."*
— Tom Dimond

This is me ...
I always pass over an offense, whether real or imagined, and free the offender of my judgement. I carry no indignation or ill will toward anyone.

Journal

Date _____

Chuckle It's what you learn after you know it all that counts.

Wisdom _"And Joseph her husband, being a righteous man and not wanting to disgrace her, planned to send her away secretly. But when he had considered this, behold, an angel of the Lord appeared to him in a dream, saying, 'Joseph son of David, do not be afraid to take Mary as your wife; for the Child who has been conceived in her is of the Holy Spirit. She will bear a Son; and you shall call His name Jesus, for He will save His people from their sins.'_
Now all this took place to fulfill what was spoken by the Lord through the prophet: 'Behold, the virgin shall be with child and shall bear a son, and they shall call his name Immanuel,' which translated means, "God with us.'"

— Matthew 1:19-23 (NASB)

This is me ...
I am so very grateful that my Father God has brought me into recovery and brought hope into the deepest pits of disaster.

Journal

Date _____

Chuckle Jim Bob and two buddies are doing a scientific study to get some party money. They're testing a new lie detector machine.

The first friend is wired to the machine and says, "I can drink for 8 days straight!" BUZZZ, the machine goes off. "Okay, 4 days straight." The machine is silent. The second is wired to the machine and says, "I can drink for six days straight!" BUZZZZZ! "Okay 3 days straight." The machine is silent.

Jim Bob is wired to the machine and says, "I think…" BUZZZZ!

Wisdom *"For this reason I kneel before the Father, from whom every family in heaven and on earth derives its name. I pray that out of his glorious riches he may strengthen you with power through his Spirit in your inner being, so that Christ may dwell in your hearts through faith. And I pray that you, being rooted and established in love, may have power, together with all the Lord's holy people, to grasp how wide and long and high and deep is the love of Christ, and to know this love that surpasses knowledge—that you may be filled to the measure of all the fullness of God. Now to him who is able to do immeasurably more than all we ask or imagine, according to his power that is at work within us, to him be glory in the church and in Christ Jesus throughout all generations, for ever and ever! Amen."*
— *Ephesians 3:14-21 (NIV)*

This is me …
I take time every day to stand still and appreciate God's many blessings, especially my loved ones and the relationships I have with them and Him.

Journal

Date _____

Chuckle Jim and Bob were sitting beside a large beer truck at a red light on an extremely hot summer day. On the side of the truck was a picture of a thirst quenching, cold looking, bottle of beer.

Jim looked at Bob and said, "Man, wouldn't you love to have one of those, dude?"

"You bet," replied Bob. "But where would we hide a whole truck?"

Wisdom _"No, is a complete sentence."_

— _Tom Dimond_

This is me ...
I accept my life just as it is each day and rejoice in it.

Journal

Date _____

Chuckle The NA speaker at the conference was droning on and on. Finally an old-timer got up and walked out. As the speaker was finishing up the old timer walked back in. After the meeting, the speaker asked the old timer where he had gone.

"I went and got a haircut," he said.

"A haircut? Why didn't you get a haircut before the meeting started?"

The old timer replied, "I didn't need one before the meeting started."

Wisdom _"So do not be ashamed to testify about our Lord, or ashamed of me his prisoner. But join with me in suffering for the gospel, by the power of God, who has saved us and called us to a holy life—not because of anything we have done but because of his own purpose and grace. This grace was given us in Christ Jesus before the beginning of time, but it has now been revealed through the appearing of our Savior, Christ Jesus, who has destroyed death and has brought life and immortality to light through the gospel."_

— _2 Timothy 1:8-11 (NIV)_

This is me ...
I am aware of the movements I make each day toward better physical, mental and spiritual health because they are made deliberately.

Journal

Date _____

Chuckle During my drinking days, my idea of a balanced diet was a full bottle of beer in each hand.

Wisdom _"If you want to make an enemy, try and change someone."_

— Tom Dimond

This is me ...
When I love unconditionally, life is so much easier.

Journal

Date _____

Chuckle This sign hangs on a liquor store: "We install and service hangovers."

Wisdom *"He is the image of the invisible God, the firstborn over all creation. For by him all things were created: things in heaven and on earth, visible and invisible, whether thrones or powers or rulers or authorities; all things were created by him and for him. He is before all things, and in him all things hold together. And he is the head of the body, the church; he is the beginning and the firstborn from among the dead, so that in everything he might have the supremacy. For God was pleased to have all his fullness dwell in him, and through him to reconcile to himself all things, whether things on earth or things in heaven, by making peace through his blood, shed on the cross."*

— Colossians 1:15-20 (NIV)

This is me ...
I am free to live eternally because of the perfect gift of Jesus Christ.

Journal

Date _____

Chuckle When things get worse faster than you can lower your standards, you may be close to your bottom.

Wisdom _"Thought—is parent to the act."_

— Jerry Moore, I love you.

This is me ...
I continually, constantly, regularly, relentlessly, repeatedly, invariably, eternally, unconditionally, unquestionably, undoubtedly, entirely, perpetually, undeniably, utterly, completely abandon myself to my loving, Father God.

Journal

Date _____

Chuckle The Serenity Prayer probably won't stop a train—so I don't park on the track.

Wisdom _"Since the children have flesh and blood, he too shared in their humanity so that by his death he might destroy him who holds the power of death—that is, the devil— and free those who all their lives were held in slavery by their fear of death. For surely it is not angels he helps, but Abraham's descendants. For this reason he had to be made like his brothers in every way, in order that he might become a merciful and faithful high priest in service to God, and that he might make atonement for the sins of the people. Because he himself suffered when he was tempted, he is able to help those who are being tempted."_

— _Hebrews 2:14-18 (NIV)_

This is me ...
I avoid anger and resentment at all costs—these toxic, deadly poisons destroy me—body and soul.

Journal

Date _____

Chuckle Jim Bob went to his therapist. "Doc," he said, "I've got trouble. Every time I go to bed, I dream that there's somebody under it. I get under the bed, then I think there's somebody on top of it. Please help me. I'm going completely nuts!"

"Just put yourself in my hands for two years,' said the shrink. "Come to me three times a week, and I'll cure you."

"How much do you charge?"

"A hundred dollars per visit."

"I'll think about it," said Jim Bob.

Three months later, the doctor met Jim Bob on the street. "Why didn't you ever come to see me again?" he asked.

"For a hundred bucks a visit? A bartender cured me for free."

"Is that so!" exclaimed the therapist. "How?"

"He told me to saw the legs off the bed."

Wisdom *"Trust the Lord with all your heart and do not lean on your own understanding; in all your ways acknowledge Him, and will make your paths straight."*

— Proverbs 3:5-6 (NIV)

This is me ...
I have discovered that hope and faith instantly turn my world into a wonderfully fragrant garden of joy and peace.

Journal

Date _____

Chuckle Second wind: That's what an NA speaker inevitably acquires when he or she says, "And now, in closing…"

Wisdom *"I have held many things in my hands, and I have lost them all; but whatever I have placed in God's hands, that I still possess."*

— Martin Luther

This is me ...
I no longer have the inclination toward revenge. It has been replaced with the full richness of forgiveness.
Ahhhhhh!

Journal

Date _____

Chuckle Since I've been sober, I no longer come to in the morning, roll over, and introduce myself.

Wisdom *"Change your thoughts and you change your world."*

— *Norman Vincent Peale*

This is me ...
God changes my thoughts as I bring the flickering flame of my humanity into contact with Him—the all-consuming fire.

Journal

Date _____

Chuckle Jim Bob went to the doctor with two burned ears. "Now how on earth did you do that?" inquired the doctor.

"Well," said Jim Bob, "I was using the iron when the phone rang and I put it to my ear by mistake."

"So, how did you burn the other ear?" the doctor asked.

"They called back," replied Jim Bob.

Wisdom _"I was created in love. For that reason nothing can express my beauty nor liberate me except love alone."_

— _Mechtild of Magdeburg_

This is me ...
I seek to perpetually give love, time and attention to those put in my path. I am a channel, bringing God's love to His children.

Journal

Date _____

Chuckle "I don't want to worry you," said the second grader to his teacher, "but my Dad says that if my grades don't improve soon, somebody is gonna' be gettin' a spankin' that they won't soon forget!"

Wisdom *"This above all, to refuse to be a victim. Unless I can do that I can do nothing."*

— *Margaret Atwood*

This is me ...
There are not victims—only voluteers. I am a hero in my life—not a victim.

Journal

Date _____

Chuckle Buying a round for the house is a great way of meeting a lot of people you can quite possibly live without.

Wisdom _"To be truly whole, I must focus on clearing away blame. And when compulsive cyclones are stirred by erratic biochemical wind-streams, I must turn to the One that calms all storms."_

— _David Rioux_

This is me ...
I will uphold the boundaries of my privacy each day and respect the right of others to do the same.

Journal

Date _____

Chuckle Jim Bob wandered unarmed into the woods and ran straight into a very hungry bear. Terrified, he fell to his knees and began praying for his life, whereupon the bear knelt down beside him.

Seeing this, Jim Bob exclaimed, "Dear brother bear! A moment ago I feared for my life, and now you join me in prayer! Oh, thank the Lord!"

"Hush," said the bear, "I'm saying grace."

Wisdom *"For this very reason, Christ died and returned to life so that he might be the Lord of both the dead and the living. You, then, why do you judge your brother? Or why do you look down on your brother? For we will all stand before God's judgment seat. It is written: 'As surely as I live,' says the Lord, 'every knee will bow before me; every tongue will confess to God.' So then, each of us will give an account of himself to God."*

— *Romans 14:9-12 (NIV)*

This is me ...
I stand before my Creator—clean, because this is how He sees me when I put my faith in His gift.
I humble myself before Him, confess all of my defects to Him, ask for His forgiveness and strength to do His will. These He gives me without reservation. He covers me with His love and protection through Jesus—who came to rescue me. I stand clean in Him.
Thank You, Jesus.

Journal

Date _____

Chuckle The biggest problem with staying home alone and isolated is that you are very likely to get a lot of bad advice.

Wisdom _"Therefore, brothers, we have an obligation—but it is not to the sinful nature, to live according to it. For if you live according to the sinful nature, you will die; but if by the Spirit you put to death the misdeeds of the body, you will live, because those who are led by the Spirit of God are sons of God. For you did not receive a spirit that makes you a slave again to fear, but you received the Spirit of sonship. And by him we cry, "Abba, Father." The Spirit himself testifies with our spirit that we are God's children. Now if we are children, then we are heirs—heirs of God and co-heirs with Christ, if indeed we share in his sufferings in order that we may also share in his glory."_

— _Romans 8:12-17 (NIV)_

This is me ...
My Father God always holds me close. He will never let me go.

Journal

Date _____

Chuckle Intoxication is feeling quite sophisticated, even when you can't pronounce it.

Wisdom *"Never pay back evil for evil to anyone. Respect what is right in the sight of all men. If possible, so far as it depends on you, be at peace with all men. Never take your own revenge, beloved, but leave room for the wrath of God, for it is written, 'Vengeance is mine, I will repay,' says the LORD. 'But if your enemy is hungry, feed him, and if he is thirsty, give him a drink; for in so doing you will heap burning coals on his head.'*

Do not be overcome by evil, but overcome evil with good."
— *Romans 12:17-21 (NASB)*

This is me ...
I strive to live at peace with everyone—this is my Father God's will for me.

Journal

Date _____

Chuckle The most dangerous tool in your kitchen is your corkscrew.

Wisdom _"To him who is able to keep you from falling and to present you before his glorious presence without fault and with great joy—to the only God our Savior be glory, majesty, power and authority, through Jesus Christ our Lord, before all ages, now and forevermore! Amen."_

— Jude 1:24-25 (NIV)

This is me ...
I am thrilled to understand that God's mercies are fresh each and every morning!

Journal

Chuckle Whenever someone says that they never drink anything stronger than pop, you might want to check and see what Pop drinks.

Wisdom *"From the 'little sins' you practice, much sorrow will accrue,*
For soon they form the habits that finally ruin you.
To avoid your downfall, this wise statement is true.
Be the master of your habits or they will master you."

— *Unknown*

This is me ...
I am successful as a human being. I overcome many challenges through meditation and prayer and the guidance that comes from above.

Journal

Date _____

Chuckle At a New Year's celebration they handed out buttons with DD written on them, standing for the Designated Drivers so that the bartender would know not to serve them. Jim Bob stumbled up to the bar, fell on his face, got up and ordered a drink.

"Aren't you a Designated Driver?" asked the bartender. "I see that you are wearing one of our DD buttons.

"No," answered Jim Bob, "I'm Dead Drunk!"

Wisdom _"For a child will be born to us, a son will be given to us; and the government will rest on His shoulders; and His name will be called Wonderful Counselor, Mighty God, Eternal Father, Prince of Peace."_

— Isaiah 9:6 (NASB)

This is me ...
The Prince of Peace is my Teacher.

Journal

Date _____

Chuckle Q: How do you get Jim Bob up on the roof? A: Tell him that the drinks are on the house!

Wisdom *"When tempted, no one should say, 'God is tempting me.' For God cannot be tempted by evil, nor does he tempt anyone; but each one is tempted when, by his own evil desire, he is dragged away and enticed. Then, after desire has conceived, it gives birth to sin; and sin, when it is full-grown, gives birth to death."*

— James 1:13-15 (NIV)

This is me ...
Today, I release my character defects to my Father God's care. He longs for me to be happy, joyous and free.

Journal

Date _____

Chuckle Jim Bob walked into a bar late at night and quickly downed six double shots. The woman on the next bar stool said, "Man, you must be really thirsty!"

"Not really," he said.

"Well, then, you must like to drink."

"Yeah" replies Jim Bob, "maybe a little."

"Well, what do you call six double shots in ten minutes?"

"Necessity," he sighs. "Yes, I have trouble with my children: every night they are out until two or three in the morning."

"What are they doing out so late?" asked the woman.

"Looking for me," said Jim Bob, sadly.

Wisdom *"Who is a God like you,*
   who pardons sin and forgives the transgression of the remnant of his inheritance?
You do not stay angry forever but delight to show mercy.
You will again have compassion on us; you will tread our sins underfoot and hurl all our iniquities into the depths of the sea."

— Micah 7:18-19 (NIV)

This is me ...
I will let go of my evil desires and seek God's perfect will for my life. He and I together will not let evil reign in me.

Journal

Chuckle Q: What do you call a psychiatrist who works in an apron? A: A bartender.

Wisdom *"A fool's anger is known at once, but a prudent man conceals dishonor."*

— *Proverbs 12:16 (NASB)*

This is me ...
I am spectacular!

Journal

Date _____

Chuckle One tequila, two tequila, three keteela, floor.

Wisdom _"So in everything, do to others what you would have them do to you, for this sums up the Law and the Prophets."_

— _Matthew 7:12 (NIV)_

This is me ...
I daily pause to seek that quiet place within, where God's peace stills the noise of life and fills my soul with heavenly delights.

Journal

Date _____

Chuckle: "A man who thinks he has no faults has at least one."

— Herbert Pronchnow

Wisdom _"If I Had My Life to Live Over…I'd relax…I would take fewer things seriously. I would take more chances. I would climb more mountains and swim more rivers…I'd start barefoot earlier in the spring and stay that way later in the fall. I would ride more merry-go-rounds. I would pick more daises."_

— Nadine Stair

This is me ...
I believe everything is going to work out perfectly according to God's will. I find growth even amidst life's trials.

Journal

Date _____

Chuckle Jim Bob enrolled in a class but didn't get along with the instructor. One day the instructor was asking philosophical questions. He asked, "If I saw a man beating a donkey and I stopped him, what virtue would I be showing?"
Jim Bob answered, "Brotherly Love."

Wisdom *"As you Think, you Travel: and as you Love, you Attract. You are today where your thoughts brought you. You cannot escape the results of your thoughts. But you can endure, accept and be glad. You will realize the vision (not the idle wish) of your heart, be it base or beautiful, or a mixture of both, for you will always gravitate toward that which you secretly love. Into your hands will be placed the exact results of your thoughts.*

You will receive that which you earned, no more—no less. Whatever your present environment may be, you will fail, remain or rise with your thoughts, your vision, your ideals. You will become as big as your dominant aspirations."

— *James Allen*

This is me ...
I entertain only positive, encouraging, uplifting and healthy thoughts. All other thoughts are deleted.

Journal

Date _____

Chuckle "Gimme another double, Charley, I'm celebrating."

"What's the occasion, Jim Bob?"

"I just finished putting a jigsaw puzzle together in only three weeks!"

"That so? How many pieces did it have?"

"Twelve!" said Jim Bob, proudly.

"Three weeks for twelve pieces— what's so great about that?"

"Well, the box said '2-3 years'!"

Wisdom _"Before destruction the heart of man is haughty, but humility goes before honor."_

— _Proverbs 18:12 (NASB)_

This is me ...

I will remain faithful and dedicated to the path toward my Father God's house, especially when the temptations, fears and pains of my transforming journey seem overwhelming.

Journal

Date _____

Chuckle There is safety in numbers. Especially numbers One through Twelve.

Wisdom *"And Jesus knowing their thoughts said, 'Why are you thinking evil in your hearts? Which is easier to say, "Your sins are forgiven," or to say, "Get up and walk"?*
'But so that you may know that the Son of Man has authority on earth to forgive sins'—then He said to the paralytic, 'Get up, pick up your bed and go home.' And he got up and went home."
— Matthew 9:4-7 (NASB)

This is me ...
I know perfectly well when I am not doing God's will because my whole being feels out of balance and unclean. But when I am in the middle of His will I feel in safe and at peace.

Journal

Date _____

Chuckle A policeman really tied one on one night, but still went to work the next morning, even though he had a terrible hangover. At noon, two other cops drove past the corner where he was in the middle of a terrible traffic jam. One cop said, "Poor idiot, he must be really hurtin' after last night." The other replied, "Yeah, but just wait till he remembers it's his day off."

Wisdom *"Let all bitterness and wrath and anger and clamor and slander be put away from you, along with all malice. Be kind to one another, tenderhearted, forgiving each other, just as God in Christ also has forgiven you."*
— *Ephesians 4:31-32 (NASB)*

This is me ...
I am kind and compassionate to each and every person I encounter. I release them from my expectations.

Journal

Date _____

Chuckle At an NA conference, a long-winded speaker began describing every detail of his life. After an hour, when the meeting was supposed to end, half the audience got up and left. However, the speaker just kept talking. A hour later, several more people left. The speaker kept right on talking. Then, everyone else—except one woman—got up and left. At last, the speaker finished up. "Oh, wow!" he said, looking out where the audience had been. "Where did everybody go?"

"You talked so long that they left," the woman replied.

"That's terrible! I had no idea I was going on so long," the speaker exclaimed. "But, why did you stay?"

"I'm the next speaker," she replied.

Wisdom _"Yes, we love peace, but we are not willing to take wounds for it, as we are for war."_

— _John Andrew Holmes_

This is me ...
I will do as Jesus commands and turn the other cheek when attacked.

Journal

Date _____

Chuckle A conceited business man tossed a street person a quarter, saying, "Here—not because you've earned it, but because it pleases me to give it to you!" "Gee thanks," cracked the panhandler. "Next time, why don't you really treat yourself and make it a buck!"

Wisdom *"I have revealed you to those whom you gave me out of the world. They were yours; you gave them to me and they have obeyed your word. Now they know that everything you have given me comes from you. For I gave them the words you gave me and they accepted them. They knew with certainty that I came from you, and they believed that you sent me. I pray for them. I am not praying for the world, but for those you have given me, for they are yours."*

— John 17:6-9 (NIV)

This is me ...
I am God's child, whom He loves.

Journal

Date _____

Chuckle One late afternoon, Jim Bob, an old stoner, wandered into the pool hall.

"Hey, Jim Bob! "Have you been smokin' dope all day?" someone asked.

Jim Bob turned slowly around with a confused look on his face, thought a minute, and replied, "I don't know, maaan. What day is it?"

Wisdom _"After the Sabbath, at dawn on the first day of the week, Mary Magdalene and the other Mary went to look at the tomb. There was a violent earthquake, for an angel of the Lord came down from heaven and, going to the tomb, rolled back the stone and sat on it. His appearance was like lightning, and his clothes were white as snow. The guards were so afraid of him that they shook and became like dead men. The angel said to the women, "Do not be afraid, for I know that you are looking for Jesus, who was crucified. He is not here; he has risen, just as he said. Come and see the place where he lay. Then go quickly and tell his disciples: 'He has risen from the dead and is going ahead of you into Galilee. There you will see him.' Now I have told you."_
— Matthew 28:1-7 (NIV)

This is me ...
I love.

Journal

Date _____

Chuckle Jim and Bob were sitting in a bar throwing back a couple dozen drinks and complaining about all of the money that they had wasted going to AA.

Jim said, "Maaan, when I think about all those dollars that I threw into the basket, and all the gas I burned up going to and from those stupid meetings where I didn't even listen to a single word that was said, what a waste."

"Yeah, maaan," said Bob. "And what about the money I blew on that AA Big Book. And I never even read it!"

"Yeah," responded Jim. "Hey, bartender, let's have another round for the house!"

"Yeah, now you're talkin'," said Bob.

Wisdom _"The wind and waves are always on the side of the ablest navigators."_

— _Edward Gibbon_

This is me ...
I never see failure as a loss. I see failure as an occasion to learn.

Journal

Date _____

Chuckle A doctor and a lawyer were visiting at a party and people were constantly interrupting the doctor and asking for free medical advice.

The doctor finally said to the lawyer, "This is so frustrating; people are always asking me for free advice. What do you do when this happens to you?"

"I give them the advice and then I send them a bill."

"That is a great idea," said the doctor.

Two days later he was opening his mail and found a bill from the lawyer.

Wisdom *"In the past God spoke to our forefathers through the prophets at many times and in various ways, but in these last days he has spoken to us by his Son, whom he appointed heir of all things, and through whom he made the universe. The Son is the radiance of God's glory and the exact representation of his being, sustaining all things by his powerful word. After he had provided purification for sins, he sat down at the right hand of the Majesty in heaven."*

— Hebrews 1:1-3 (NIV)

This is me ...
My time here on earth is short. I look forward to visiting other worlds and galaxies. I do love to travel and am very excited to see the rest of the universe.

Journal

Date _____

Chuckle Two acid freaks were laying on the beach one night, trippin'. One said to the other, "How many moons do you see tonight, maaan?"

"Wow, that's deep, maaan," the other replied. "In which color, maaan?"

Wisdom _"To see, we must stop being in the middle of the picture."_

— _Satprem._

This is me ...
There is a place deep within me that knows—I am straining toward the heights of perfection my Creator wishes for me to enjoy, for His glory—not mine.

Journal

Date _____

Chuckle Jim Bob was sitting in a bar getting pie-eyed. After each drink he would take a picture out of his pocket, look at it for a minute, put it back and continue drinking. Finally, the bartender couldn't stand it anymore.

"Excuse me, sir," he asked, "you've been doing that all night—who's the photo of?"

"My wife," he explained.
"Oh, sorry, did she…pass away?"

"No."

"Then why do you keep looking at her picture?"

"When she starts looking good," Jim Bob replied, "it's time for me to quit and go home."

Wisdom _"Do not forget to entertain strangers, for by so doing some people have entertained angels without knowing it. Remember those in prison as if you were their fellow prisoners, and those who are mistreated as if you yourselves were suffering."_
— Hebrews 13:2-3 (NASB)

This is me …
I fear nothing except the absence of my Father God. I will strive to not push Him away.

Journal

Date _____

Chuckle The Friday night speaker at the NA convention walked up to the podium, looked out at the stadium full of people and said, "My heart is pounding, my knees are weak, my mouth is bone dry, my stomach is in knots, I feel nervous and scared.
I used to pay a lot of money for this feeling."

Wisdom _"Be gracious to me, O God, according to Your loving kindness; according to the greatness of Your compassion, blot out my transgressions. Wash me thoroughly from my iniquity and cleanse me from my sin."_

— _Psalm 51:1-2 (NASB)_

This is me ...
I love to stand in my Father God's presence for His light makes the darkness flee. I will live in His light.

Journal

Date _____

Chuckle When I asked my sponsor if it was alright for me to go to the bars to see my friends and just drink soda he replied, "You know, Jim Bob, if you go to the Barber Shop every day to read the newspaper, sooner or later you are going to get a hair cut."

Wisdom *"After He called the crowd to Him again, He began saying to them, 'Listen to Me, all of you, and understand: there is nothing outside the man which can defile him if it goes into him; but the things which proceed out of the man are what defile the man. If anyone has ears to hear, let him hear.'"*

— *Mark 7:14-15 (NASB)*

This is me ...
As I walk daily with my Creator, enjoying His presence—the desire to do good and speak positively expands.

Journal

Date _____

Chuckle Three college coeds were getting undressed in the locker room when someone knocked on the door.

"Who is it?" one of the coeds asked.

"The blind man" came the response.

So, she decided to let him in because he was blind.

A handsome young man walked in and said, "Wow, you girls are beautiful and very, very friendly. Where do you want me to install these blinds?"

Wisdom *"Therefore, since we have so great a cloud of witnesses surrounding us, let us also lay aside every encumbrance and the sin which so easily entangles us, and let us run with endurance the race that is set before us, fixing our eyes on Jesus, the author and perfecter of faith, who for the joy set before Him endured the cross, despising the shame, and has sat down at the right hand of the throne of God. For consider Him who has endured such hostility by sinners against Himself, so that you will not grow weary and lose heart."*

— Hebrews 12:1-3 (NASB)

This is me ...
I dearly appreciate the discipline of my Father God, even though, at times, it might seem harsh.

Journal

Date _____

Chuckle An old stoner was fishing. When he caught a fish he'd put it in a bucket of water. As he was leaving the lake with two buckets full of live fish a game warden stopped him. "Got a fishing license?" the warden asked.

"No way, maaan," the hippie replied. "I would never catch fish, maaan, that's cruel. These are my pet fish."

"Pet fish?" the warden exclaimed.

"Yeah, maan," he explained. "Every night I take these fish down to the lake and let them swim around for a while. Then I whistle and they jump back into their buckets, and I take 'em home."

"I don't believe that!" said the warden. "Fish can't do that!"

The hippie smiled for a second and said, "Here, I'll show you."

"Okay," said the warden. "I've got to see this."

So they walked back to the edge of the lake and the hippie poured the fish into the water, then stood back and waited. Several minutes went by, and the warden was getting impatient.

"Well?" he asked.

"Well, what?" replied the stoner.

"When are you going to call them back?" the warden demanded.

"Call who back?" asked the stoner.

"The fish!" said the warden.

"What fish?" asked the hippie.

Wisdom _"I shall tell you a great secret, my friend. Do not wait for the last judgment, it takes place every day."_
— _Albert Camus_

This is me ...
I do not know when my last day on earth will be. If I were to treat this day as my last, what would I make sure to get done?

Journal

Date _____

Chuckle Jim Bob went to church and as he was leaving the minister grabbed his hand at the door and said. "Jim Bob, you need to be in the Lord's army."

Jim Bob answered, "I am in the Lord's army."

"Then why do I only see you at Christmas and Easter?" asked the minister.

Jim Bob looked around discretely and whispered in the minister's ear, "I'm in the Secret Service."

Wisdom _"Man's way leads to a hopeless end; God's way leads to an endless hope."_

— _Anonymous_

This is me ...
I have walked through the darkness into the light. I will not turn back.

Journal

Date _____

Chuckle Jim Bob was at a tavern enjoying a beer when suddenly the door burst open and someone shouted, "Run for your lives! Big Jake's comin'!"

As everyone scattered, an enormous man crashed through the door, kicked tables and chairs aside, and strode up to the bar. "Gimme a drink," he ordered.

Jim Bob quickly handed over a bottle of whiskey. The huge man drank the whole bottle and smashed it against the wall behind the bar.

Shaking with fear, Jim Bob said, "Can I get you another?"

"Nope, I gotta go," growled the giant. "Didn't you hear? Big Jake is comin'!"

Wisdom _"The Holy Spirit also testifies to us about this. First he says: 'This is the covenant I will make with them after that time, says the Lord._
I will put my laws in their hearts, and I will write them on their minds.'
Then he adds: 'Their sins and lawless acts I will remember no more.'"

— _Hebrews 10:15-17 (NIV)_

This is me ...
I will keep my heart open to the voice of my Father God.

Journal

Date _____

Chuckle The condemned man was blindfolded, and put against the wall.

The captain of the firing squad asked him, "Cigarette?"

Criminal: "I don't smoke."

Captain: "Rum?"

Criminal: "No thanks, I've almost got ninety days sober."

Wisdom *"Therefore, since we have a great high priest who has passed through the heavens, Jesus the Son of God, let us hold fast our confession. For we do not have a high priest who cannot sympathize with our weaknesses, but One who has been tempted in all things as we are, yet without sin. Therefore let us draw near with confidence to the throne of grace, so that we may receive mercy and find grace to help in time of need."*

— Hebrews 4:14-16 (NASB)

This is me ...
I can go there—you know—that uncomfortable place where all of my character defects are left behind and only goodness dwells. It is safe for me to be there because God is there.

Journal

Date _____

Chuckle The police officer had just handed him a ticket. But the crack-head was belligerent.

"What am I supposed to do with this?" he demanded.

"Keep it," the police officer replied. "When you collect five of them, you get a free room and board from the State."

Wisdom *"May the God of hope fill you with all joy and peace as you trust in him, so that you may overflow with hope by the power of the Holy Spirit."*
— Romans 15:13 (NIV)

This is me ...
I am overflowing with the fruit of God's Spirit—love, joy, peace, patience, kindness, goodness, faithfulness, gentleness and self-control.

Journal

Date _____

Chuckle Jim Bob was in jail as a suspect in a daring casino robbery. He got a letter from his wife who asked him when she was supposed to plant the garden. Since Jim Bob knew that the jailer read all mail he wrote back, saying, "Stay out of the garden. I buried the money that I stole from the casino in there."

A couple of days later he got another letter from his wife saying: "You won't believe it, Jim Bob. The sheriff came with a dozen men and they dug up the entire garden." Jim Bob wrote back: "Now you can plant."

Wisdom *"This is what the Lord says: 'Let not he wise boast of their wisdom or the strong boast of their strength or the rich boast of their riches, but let those who boast boast about this: that they understand and know me, that I am the LORD, who exercises kindness, justice and righteousness on the earth, for in these I delight' declares the LORD.'"*

— Jeremiah 9:23-24 (TNIV)

This is me ...
I am free.

Journal

Date _____

Chuckle A down n' out crackhead was looking for ways to come up with some quick cash and spotted a mean-looking old man sweeping the sidewalk in front of his store.

"Do you have any old beer bottles?" the tweeker asked him.

Self-righteously, he said, "Do I look like the sort of person who would drink beer?"

"Excuse me," apologized the tweeker. "Any old vinegar bottles!"

Wisdom _"It is shameful even to mention what the disobedient do in secret. But everything exposed by the light becomes visible—and everything that is illuminated becomes a light. This is why it is said: 'Wake up, sleeper, rise from the dead and Christ will shine on you.'"_

— _Ephesians 5:12-14 (TNIV)_

This is me ...
God has awakened me. I will not join the walking dead again. I will expose all darkness in me to His consuming light.

Journal

Date _____

Chuckle Jim and Bob were out golfing one day. Jim was ready to tee off. He kept looking up at the club house while preparing his swing. Bob finally blurted out, "What is taking you so long?"

Jim replied, "My wife is in the club house watching me. I want  to make a perfect shot."

Bob shook his head and said, "Man, you don't have a chance of hitting her from here."

Wisdom _"Therefore, I urge you, brothers and sisters, in view of God's mercy, to offer your bodies as a living sacrifice, holy and pleasing to God— this is true worship. Do not conform to the pattern of this world, but be transformed by the renewing of your mind. Then you will be able to test and approve what God's will is—his good, pleasing and perfect will. For by the grace given me I say to everyone of you: Do not think of yourself more highly that you ought, but rather think of yourself with sober judgment, in accordance with the faith God has distributed to each of you."_

— Romans 12:1-3 (TNIV)

This is me ...
I am just house sitting in this tired old body. I will move on someday to a permanent, heavenly body that will never get sick, wear out or die.

Journal

Date _____

Chuckle Jim Bob got work at a construction site. After an hour or so, the boss yelled at him, "Hey, everyone else is carrying eight bricks—how come you're only carrying four?"

"I don't know," replied Jim Bob, "maybe they're just too lazy to make two trips."

Wisdom _"I have great confidence in you; I take great pride in you. I am greatly encouraged; in all our troubles my joy knows no bounds."_

— _2 Corinthians 7:4 (NIV)_

This is me ...
My life is beautiful!

Journal

Date _____

Chuckle One night while out partying, I had to drag my wife out of the bar and force her to go home. Unfortunately it wasn't until the next morning that I remembered that I wasn't even married.

Wisdom *"When Jesus spoke again to the people, he said, 'I am the light of the world. Whoever follows me will never walk in darkness, but will have the light of life.'"*

— *John 8:12 (TNIV)*

This is me ...
Deep within the inner most part of me there resides a strength that can not be disturbed or shaken. It is the power of God deposited within me through His Holy Spirit. He gives me the ability to face any storm with assurance and trust.

Journal

Date _____

Chuckle Jim Bob was sitting in a dark corner of the bar when a woman came up the him and said, "Hello, good-looking. I'll do anything you want for a hundred dollars."

"Are you serious?"

"Absolutely, baby, anything you want."

"Alright, then let's go!"

"Oooohhh! You are eager, honey, what did you have in mind?"

"I want you to paint my house."

Wisdom *"For the LORD gives wisdom, and from his mouth come knowledge and understanding. He holds victory in store for the upright, he is a shield to those whose walk is blameless, for he guards the course of the just and protects the way of his faithful ones. Then you will understand what is right and just and fair—every good path. For wisdom will enter your heart, and knowledge will be pleasant to your soul. Discretion will protect you, and understanding will guard you. Wisdom will save you from the ways of wicked men, from men whose words are perverse, who leave the straight paths to walk in dark ways . . ."*

— Proverbs 2:6-13 (NIV)

This is me ...
If I am not clean and sober—I loose.

Journal

Date _____

Chuckle There may not be a fountain of youth, but a couple of drinks sure does make almost everybody act a lot less mature.

Wisdom _"Do not be wise in your own eyes; fear the LORD and shun evil. This will bring health to your body and nourishment to your bones. Honor the LORD with your wealth, with the firstfruits of all your crops; then your barns will be filled to overflowing, and your vats will brim over with new wine."_

— _Proverbs 3:7-10 (NIV)_

This is me ...
I am not proud or rude. I am patient and kind. I am not self-seeking or easily angered. I walk in God's love.

Journal

Date _____

Chuckle Jim Bob moved from New York City to Oregon and decided to become a logger. He bought a top-of-the-line chain saw and went to work. Frustrated, he returned to the store and told the salesman, "This chain saw is a piece of junk. It took me all day to cut down one small tree!" The salesman took the saw and started it up.

Jim Bob jumped back and said, "What's that noise!"

Wisdom _"Blessed are the poor in spirit, for theirs is the kingdom of heaven. Blessed are those who mourn, for they will be comforted. Blessed are the meek, for they will inherit the earth. Blessed are those who hunger and thirst for righteousness, for they will be filled. Blessed are the merciful, for they will be shown mercy. Blessed are the pure in heart, for they will see God. Blessed are the peacemakers, for they will be called sons of God. Blessed are those who are persecuted because of righteousness, for theirs is the kingdom of heaven."_

— Matthew 5:3-10 (NIV)

This is me ...
I am blessed. I will continually focus on the joys of life.

Journal

Date _____

Chuckle If you need to have the last word in an argument, try saying, "I guess you're right."

Wisdom _"On hearing this, Jesus said, 'It is not the healthy who need a doctor, but the sick. But go and learn what this means: I desire mercy, not sacrifice. For I have not come to call the righteous, but sinners.'"_

— Matthew 9:12-13 (TNIV)

This is me ...
I come to the Great Physician for healing. He knows the end from the beginning and He alone knows the best path for me. He has my eternal interest in mind. I trust Him even when He says "no" or "not now."

Journal

Date _____

Chuckle: Jim Bob staggered home about dinner time. As his wife Helen was cooking over a hot stove she asked him if he wanted dinner. "What are my choices?" he replied. She looked at him and sarcastically said, "Yes, or No."

Wisdom _"'Truly I tell you, if you say to this mountain, "Go, throw yourself into the sea," and do not doubt in your heart but believe that what you say will happen, it will be done for you. Therefore I tell you, whatever you ask for in prayer, believe that you have received it, and it will be yours. And when you stand praying, if you hold anything against anyone, forgive him, so that your Father in heaven may forgive you your sins.'"_

— Mark 11:23-26 (TNIV)

This is me ...
The God of heaven, the Creator of earth is my Higher Power. He is absolutely the Highest Power in the universe.

Journal

Date _____

Chuckle Jim Bob was a little slow after all his years of drinking. His boss came into his office one day, saying: "Jim Bob, we have decided that you shouldn't take any more coffee breaks."

"Why on earth not?" demanded Jim Bob.

The boss answered, "We are getting tired of retraining you."

Wisdom _"'No good tree bears bad fruit, nor does a bad tree bear good fruit. Each tree is recognized by its own fruit. People do not pick figs from thorn bushes, or grapes from briers. Good people bring good things out of the good stored up in their heart, and evil people bring evil things out of the evil stored up in their heart. For out of the overflow of the heart the mouth speaks.'"_

— _Luke 6:43-45 (TNIV)_

This is me ...
I will bear good fruit in my llife. I will speak good words to all and about all.

Journal

Date _____

Chuckle Jim Bob got into a drunken fight at the bar. When he got home and saw that his face was pretty cut up. He attempted to cover the damage the best he could with band-aids.

Helen came in the next morning woke him up. "You were drunk and fighting again last night, weren't you."

Jim Bob looked at her indignantly and answered: "Absolutely not! I had to work late and I stopped for a drink or two with the boys. I simply fell down the stairs and scratched my face. Why do you always assume that I get drunk when I go out?"

Helen responded: "Well, idiot, my first clue was the band-aids all over the mirror."

Wisdom *"Out of suffering have emerged the strongest souls; the most massive characters are seared with scars."*
— E. H. Chapin

This is me ...
I don't have a religion. I have a spiritual program of recovery. I have the One true God! He has set me free from all bondage. He is not a religion. He is a reality.

Journal

Date _____

Chuckle Jim Bob drove out of the parking lot of the bar and hit a parked car while a dozen people watched him. Fearing he would be reported for hit-and- run, he pulled over got out and wrote this note: "A dozen people saw me hit your car and think that I am giving you my name and phone number."

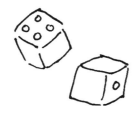

Wisdom *"God doesn't play dice."*
— *Albert Einstein*

This is me ...
Adversity introduced me to my God. I am grateful for the pain.

Journal

Date _____

Chuckle: Jim and Bob were having a drink or two or three and Jim was complaining about how much his wife took him for granted. He turned to Bob and said, "My wife just doesn't appreciate me Bob. Does yours?" Bob thought for a minute and responded. "I don't know Jim. I've never heard her mention your name."

Wisdom _"The LORD is my shepherd, I shall not be in want. He makes me lie down in green pastures, he leads me beside quiet waters, he restores my soul. He guides me in paths of righteousness for his name's sake. Even though I walk through the valley of the shadow of death, I will fear no evil, for you are with me; your rod and your staff, they comfort me. You prepare a table before me in the presence of my enemies. You anoint my head with oil; my cup overflows. Surely goodness and love will follow me all the days of my life, and I will dwell in the house of the LORD forever."_

— _Psalm 23 (NIV)_

This is me ...
The Lord is my Shepherd. I shall not be in want. He restores my soul.

Journal

Date _____

Chuckle Jim Bob was on a cruise when a hurricane suddenly came upon the ship. As the passengers were gathered on the deck the captain asked, "Does anyone here know how to pray."

Jim Bob replied, "I do, Captain."

"Great," said the captain. "You pray while the rest of us put on our life jackets. We're one short."

Wisdom _"Let someone else praise you, and not your own mouth; an outsider, and not your own lips."_

— _Proverbs 27:2 (TNIV)_

This is me ...
Even when I fail, I will never let go of my faith and trust in God. No matter how bad my day is, or how ugly my behavior is—He will never leave me.

Journal

Date _____

Chuckle The lady chairing the meeting called on a younger member to share.

She said, "Wow what a train wreck of a day. I was off center. I felt withdrawn. The deprived child within me was depressed. I didn't achieve any level of self-actualization!"

An old-timer who was hard of hearing leaned over and whispered to a friend, "What did she say?"

She whispered back, "She says she's hungry, angry, lonely, and tired."

Wisdom _"So I tell you this, and insist on it in the Lord, that you must no longer live as the Gentiles do, in the futility of their thinking. They are darkened in their understanding and separated from the life of God because of the ignorance that is in them due to the hardening of their hearts. Having lost all sensitivity, they have given themselves over to sensuality so as to indulge in every kind of impurity, with a continual lust for more."_
— _Ephesians 4:17, 18 (NIV)_

This is me ...
I love God with all my heart and seek His will with passion.
Therefore, my mind is filled with good, honest and honorable thoughts.

Journal

Date _____

Chuckle In our twenties, we worry about what others think of us. In our forties, we don't care what they think of us. In our sixties, we discover that they haven't been thinking of us at all.

Wisdom _"Do what you can, with what you have, where you are."_

— _Theodore Roosevelt_

This is me ...
I have learned to pay attention to what is going on at this moment. Now, is where life really happens.
As I investigate God's creation, I discover that this is a totally amazing world!

Journal

Date _____

Chuckle A woman was complaining that her husband came home drunk and late on a regular basis.

"I know how to stop that," responded her friend. My husband used to do that, but I cured him very quickly."

"How?" asked the woman.

Her friend answered. "One morning he came staggering in at three in the morning and I called out from the bedroom. Is that you Jim?"

"How could that cure him?" she asked.

"His name is Bob."

Wisdom _"Then he opened their minds so they could understand the Scriptures. He told them, 'This is what is written: The Christ will suffer and rise from the dead on the third day, and repentance and forgiveness of sins will be preached in his name to all nations, beginning at Jerusalem.'"_
— Luke 24:45-47 (TNIV)

This is me ...
I close the door to impure imaginations and unworthy thoughts by lifting my soul into God's presence and shifting my focus to Him.

Journal

Date _____

Chuckle Many times I went out for an eye-opener and came home blind.

Wisdom _"'I tell you, whoever publicly acknowledges me, the Son of Man will also acknowledge before the angels of God. But he whoever publicly disowns me will be disowned before the angels of God.'"_

— _Luke 12:8,9 (TNIV)_

This is me ...
When God said, "I will never leave you," He spoke the truth.

Journal

Date _____

Chuckle Jim Bob was once again dragged before the judge on charges of public drunkenness. When the judge asked if he pleaded guilty or not guilty, he responded.

"I definitely am not drunk, your highness, and you can spell that with a capital 'T'."

Wisdom _"Those who wish to sing, always find a song."_

— _Unknown_

This is me ...
Recovery is a process of continual action. There is no safe place where I can sit and do nothing.
When I am not involved in the actions of recovery, I am on my way to relapse.

Journal

Date _____

Chuckle Jim Bob walked into an upscale restaurant and ordered six very expensive cocktails. The waitress served them on a silver tray. Jim Bob proceeded to down them, one after another, in less than a minute.

"My word, sir," whispered the waitress, "you must have a very serious problem!"

"If you had what I have," Jim Bob whispered back, "you'd drink fast, too."

"What do you have sir?" asked the waitress.

"Fifty cents," answered Jim Bob

Wisdom _Jesus said to her, "I am the resurrection and the life. Anyone who believes in me will live, even though they die; and whoever lives and believes in me will never die. Do you believe this?"_

— _John 11: 25-26 (TNIV)_

This is me ...
I face adversity with confidence, hope and trust. It often teaches me the most valuable lessons.

Journal

Date _____

Chuckle Jim and Bob were out drinking one night when they ran out of booze and money, so they decided to steal some bottles of wine from Jim's neighbor.

As they ran away from the house, Jim turned to Bob and said, "Hey, Bob, if you can guess how many bottles we took, I'll let you drink both of them."

Bob thought for a minute and guessed, "Five?"

Wisdom *"On the last and greatest day of the Festival, Jesus stood and said in a loud voice, 'Let anyone who is thirsty come to me and drink. Whoever believes in me, as Scripture has said, rivers of living water will flow from within them.'"*

— *John 7:37-38 (TNIV)*

This is me ...
Every time I seek God's will I find that I make the right choices.

Journal

Date _____

Chuckle If a tree falls in the forest and there is no one around to hear it, does it still make a noise?
If a drunk says something in a forest, and his wife isn't there to hear him, is he still wrong?

Wisdom _"A person who is looking for something doesn't travel very fast."_

— E. B. White

This is me ...
When I slow down I usually find what I am looking for.

Journal

Date _____

Chuckle After a severe car crash Jim Bob had to visit a chiropractor regularly. After several visits and seeing that Jim Bob was not getting any better, the Doctor said, "I'm not quite sure what is wrong with you. I think it may be the drinking."
"Okay then," said Jim Bob. "Can we get an opinion from a doctor who's sober?"

Wisdom *"Be very careful, then, how you live—not as unwise but as wise, making the most of every opportunity, because the days are evil. Therefore do not be foolish, but understand what the Lord's will is. Do not get drunk on wine, which leads to debauchery. Instead, be filled with the Spirit."*
— *Ephesians 5:15-18 (TNIV)*

This is me ...
I am seriously thrilled about the prospect of being in the service of my wonderful Father God—forever.

Journal

Date _____

Chuckle It's a lot easier to get older than wiser.

Wisdom *"For it is not those who hear the law who are righteous in God's sight, but it is those who obey the law who will be declared righteous. (Indeed, when Gentiles, who do not have the law, do by nature things required by the law, they are a law for themselves, even though they do not have the law. They show that the requirements of the law are written on their hearts, their consciences also bearing witness, and their thoughts now accusing, now even defending them.) This will take place on the day when God will judge everyone's secrets through Jesus Christ, as my gospel declares."*

— *Romans 2:13-16 (TNIV)*

This is me ...
I am grateful for the rewards of each day as I continue to awaken spiritually.

Journal  Date _____

Chuckle Jim Bob stumbled up to the bar, ordered a martini, held it carefully with both hands, downed it quickly in one gulp, then ordered another and drank it the same way.

Then he ordered another.

The bartender asked, "What is with you, man, why do you drink like that?"

Jim Bob said, "I had a horrible accident and I have been drinking them like this ever since."

"What, did you have a car wreck?"

"No" replied Jim Bob, "I spilled a martini!"

Wisdom *"Two are better than one, because they have a good return for their labor: If they fall down, they can help each other up. But pity those who fall and have no one to help them up! Also, if two lie down together, they will keep warm. But how can one keep warm alone? Though one may be overpowered, two can defend themselves. A cord of three strands is not quickly broken."*

— *Ecclesiastes 4:9-12 (TNIV)*

This is me ...
I am reliable.

Journal

Date _____

Chuckle Stress is when you wake up screaming and realize that you haven't fallen asleep yet!

Wisdom *"This is how we know what love is: Jesus Christ laid down his life for us. And we ought to lay down our lives for one another. If anyone has material possessions and sees his brother in need but has no pity on them, how can the love of God be in you? Dear children, let us not love with words or tongue but with actions and in truth. This then is how we know that we belong to the truth, and how we set our hearts at rest in his presence: If our hearts condemn us, we know that God is greater than our hearts, and he knows everything. Dear friends, if our hearts do not condemn us, we have confidence before God and receive from him anything we ask, because we obey his commands and do what pleases him. And this is his command: to believe in the name of his Son, Jesus Christ, and to love one another as he commanded us. Those who obey his commands live in him, and he in them. And this is how we know that he lives in us: We know it by the Spirit he gave us."*

— *1 John 3:16-24 (TNIV)*

This is me ...
"Love and tolerance" is my code of conduct.

Journal

Date _____

Chuckle Jim Bob staggered bleary-eyed into a dark bar. His eyes focused a little and he spotted the only woman in the bar. He stumbled over to her and gave her a big kiss. She pulled away and slapped his face. He apologized slurring: "I'm so sorry. I thought you were my wife! You look just like her."

She gave him a mean look and said: "Why, you stupid, filthy, worthless, drunken idiot!"

"Wow," said Jim Bob. "You sound just like her, too!"

Wisdom *"We know that we are children of God, and that the whole world is under the control of the evil one. We know also that the Son of God has come and has given us understanding, so that we may know him who is true. And we are in him who is true by being in his son Jesus Christ. He is the true God and eternal life. Dear children, keep yourselves from idols."*

— 1 John 5:19-21 (TNIV)

This is me ...
I am related to the King of the universe.

Journal

Chuckle A very small pony walked into a bar and in a small, quiet, raspy voice ordered a drink. "I can't hear you," bellowed the bartender.

"I'm sorry," replied the pony, "I'm a little horse."

Wisdom *"Everything has its wonders, even darkness and silence, and I learn, whatever state I may be in, therein to be content."*

— *Helen Keller*

This is me ...
If I'm driving down a country road and see a turtle sitting on a fence post, I know he had a lot of help getting there. God lifts me.

Journal

Date _____

Chuckle A young alcoholic lawyer from Los Angeles went bird hunting in Texas. A bird he shot fell into a farmers' field, so he climbed the fence to get it. As he crossed the field, the farmer came out and asked what he was doing. The lawyer explained, and the farmer said, "Well, sonny, this is my land; that makes the bird mine, too."
The lawyer got angry and said. "I'm a lawyer, old timer, and if you don't give me that bird, I'll sue and this will be my farm."
   "Well, sonny," said the farmer, "we settle disputes differently here in Texas. We use the three-kick rule."
   "What is that?" asked the lawyer.
   The farmer replied. "We take turns kicking each other three times and the first one to give up is the loser."
   "Okay, old timer, take your best shot."
   The farmer kicked the lawyer between the legs, in the face as he went down, and in the belly when he hit the ground.
   The young lawyer staggered to his feet. "Alright, you old fart, it's my turn."
   "No," says the farmer. "I give up, you can have the bird."

Wisdom *"Whoever has my commands and keeps them is the one who loves me. Anyone who loves me will be loved by my Father, and I too will love them and show myself to them."*
                      — John 14:20-21 (TNIV)

This is me ...
As I gaze into a star lit night, I am marveled at the immense power of my Creator God.

Journal

Date _____

Chuckle Warning: The consumption of alcohol may cause you to thay shings like thish.

Wisdom _"But whatever were gains to me I now consider loss for the sake of Christ. What is more, I consider everything a loss because of the surpassing worth of knowing Christ Jesus my Lord, for whose sake I have lost all things._

I consider them garbage, that I may gain Christ and be found in him, not having a righteousness of my own that comes from the law, but that which is through faith in Christ—the righteousness that comes from God on the basis of faith.

I want to know Christ—yes, to know the power of his resurrection and participation in his sufferings, becoming like him in his death, and so, somehow, attaining to the resurrection from the dead."

— _Philippians 3:7-11 (TNIV)_

This is me ...
My name is servant.

Journal

Date _____

Chuckle Jim Bob once again stood before the judge, swaying back and forth and smelling of gin. The judge shouted, "Look at what you've become, Jim Bob! You are an educated man, but you live like a bum; you have lost all of your family and friends; you're hopeless, jobless and in jail. Don't you know that alcohol is responsible for your ruin?"

Jim Bob replies, "Thank you for saying so, your honor. Everybody else thinks it's my fault!"

Wisdom _"It is written: 'I believed; therefore I have spoken.' Since we have that same spirit of faith we also believe and therefore speak, because we know that the one who raised the Lord Jesus from the dead will also raise us with Jesus and present us with you to himself."_

— _2 Corinthians 4:13-14 (TNIV)_

This is me ...
My daily life is a testimony to the purity of my God and His influence in me.

Journal

Date _____

Chuckle AA poetry:
Once I was happy and I had a good wife. I had enough money to last me for life.
But I met a lady and we went on a spree. We started to smokin' and a drinkin' whiskey.
Now I'm in AA and my life has been A bed full of roses, with some manure thrown in.

Wisdom *"Listen, I tell you a mystery: We will not all sleep, but we will all be changed—in a flash, in the twinkling of an eye, at the last trumpet. For the trumpet will sound, the dead will be raised imperishable, and will be changed. For the perishable must clothe itself with the imperishable, and the mortal with immortality. When the perishable has been clothed with the imperishable, and the mortal with immortality, then the saying that is written will come true: "Death has been swallowed up in victory."
Where, O death, is your victory? Where, O death, is your sting?
The sting of death is sin, and the power of sin is the law. But thanks be to God!
He gives us the victory through our Lord Jesus Christ."*
— 1 Corinthians 15:51-57 (TNIV)

This is me ...
In giving I receive, and more abundantly.

Journal

Date _____

Chuckle A crisis is when you can't say, "Thy will be done."

Wisdom _"Stop judging others, and you will not be judged. Stop criticizing others, or it will all come back on you. If you forgive others, you will be forgiven. If you give, you will receive. Your gift will return to you in full measure, pressed down, shaken together to make room for more, and running over. Whatever measure you use in giving—large or small—it will be used to measure what is given back to you."_

— Luke 6:37-38 (NLT)

This is me ...
I am forgiven.

Journal

Date _____

Chuckle Jim and Bob were at their usual watering hole having a drink or two or three when Jim said: "The wife and I had another knock down drag out fight last night."

"Who won?" asked Bob.

"Well, let me put it this way: when it was all over, she came crawling to me on her hands and knees."

"Way to go, Jim. What did she say?" asked Bob.

She said, "Come out from under that bed, you worthless, drunken coward!"

Wisdom _"Whatever you do, work at it with all your heart, as working for the Lord, not for men, since you know that you will receive an inheritance from the Lord as a reward. It is the Lord Christ you are serving"_

— _Colossians 3:23-24(TNIV)_

This is me ...
I will receive an inheritance from the Lord that will last forever.

Journal

Date _____

Chuckle I said "no" to drugs, but they just wouldn't listen.

Wisdom *"Honesty without compassion and understanding is not honesty, but subtle hostility."*
— Rose N. Franzblau

This is me ...
When I am bored, I am boring.

Chuckle After spending hours drinking beer and explaining the theory of evolution to his Dad, the wise Father turned to Jim Bob and replied: "Son, it is often better to sit quietly and have people think that you are a fool than to open your mouth and remove all doubt."

Wisdom *"You, my brothers, were called to be free. But do not use your freedom to indulge the sinful nature; rather, serve one another humbly in love. For the entire law is fulfilled in this one command: 'Love your neighbor as yourself.'"*

— Galatians 5:13-14 (TNIV)

This is me ...
When I'm thinking of and doing things for others, my character defects have less of an influence over me.

Journal

Date _____

Chuckle Attempting to teach him about the evils of alcohol, Jim Bob's dad poured a glass of water and a glass of vodka, then dropped a live worm into each one. The worm that he dropped into the water lived, but the worm that he dropped into the vodka immediately shriveled up and died. "Alright, Jim Bob, what does that show you?"

"If you drink alcohol," Jim Bob answered, "then you won't have worms."

Wisdom *"Then he went down to Capernaum, a town in Galilee, and on the Sabbath he taught the people. They were amazed at his teaching, because his words had authority.*

In the synagogue there was a man possessed by a demon, an evil spirit. He cried out at the top of his voice, "Go away! What do you want with us, Jesus of Nazareth? Have you come to destroy us? I know who you are—the Holy One of God!"

"Be quiet!" Jesus said sternly. "Come out of him!"

Then the demon threw the man down before them all and came out without injuring him. All the people were amazed and said to each other, "What words these are! With authority and power he gives orders to evil spirits and they come out!"

— *Luke 4:31-36 (TNIV)*

This is me ...
God has commanded the demons to leave me. I will let them go.

Journal

Chuckle The old half-baked hippie went to the police station to speak with the thief who had broken into his house the night before.

"You'll get to speak to him after court," said the policeman.

"Hey, maaan, I don't care that the dude broke into my house and stole my stuff maaan. I want to know how he got in without waking my wife up. I've been trying to do that forever, maaan."

Wisdom *"There is one body and one Spirit—just as you were called to one hope when you were called—one Lord, one faith, one baptism; one God and Father of all, who is over all and through all and in all.*

But to each one of us grace has been given as Christ apportioned it. This is why it says:

'When he ascended on high, he led captives in his train and gave gifts to men.'"

— Epheisans 4:4-8 (NIV)

This is me ...
God has granted me special gifts and set me free to use them.

Journal

Date _____

Chuckle Jim Bob decided to take the bus home from the bar. As he staggered down the isle, a disgusted woman looked down her nose at him and said: "You sad, drunken man. Don't you know that you are going straight to hell?"

"Oh man," Jim Bob said, "I've taken the wrong bus!"

Wisdom *"Tire not of new beginnings: build your life, not on regret, but always upon resolve! Shed no tear on the blotted page of the past, but turn the leaf—and smile—to see the clean white page before thee."*

— *Unknown*

This is me ...
It works best for me when I pause and consider my options in that moment between someone else's action and my reaction.

Journal

Date _____

Chuckle   Jim Bob gets his dream job. On the day that he gets his first paycheck, he walks up to his boss and quits. "You're quitting already, Jim Bob? I thought that you really wanted the opportunity that we have given you here."

Jim Bob replied: "Well, I thought that I wanted a career. As it turns out, I just wanted a paycheck."

Wisdom   _"You may never know that God is all you need, until God is all you've got."_

—_Unknown_

This is me ...
God is all I will ever need.

Journal

Date _____

Chuckle Bumper sticker on Jim Bob's car: "Don't drink and drive; you might spill it."

Wisdom *"As for you, you were dead in your transgressions and sins, in which you used to live when you followed the ways of this world and of the ruler of the kingdom of the air, the spirit who is now at work in those who are disobedient. All of us also lived among them at one time, gratifying the cravings of our sinful nature and following its desires and thoughts. Like the rest, we were by nature deserving of wrath. But because of his great love for us, God, who is rich in mercy, made us alive with Christ even when we were dead in transgressions—it is by grace you have been saved. And God raised us up with Christ and seated us with him in the heavenly realms in Christ Jesus, in order that in the coming ages he might show the incomparable riches of his grace, expressed in his kindness to us in Christ Jesus. For it is by grace you have been saved, through faith— and this not from yourselves, it is the gift of God—not by works, so that no one can boast. For we are God's handiwork, created in Christ Jesus to do good works, which God prepared in advance for us to do."*
— *Ephesians 2:1-10 (TNIV)*

This is me ...
I make room for spiritual progress daily.

Journal

Date _____

Chuckle At daybreak one morning, a cop found Jim Bob staggering around downtown and asked, "Can you explain why you're out at this hour?" "If I could," Jim Bob replied, "I'd be home by now."

Wisdom _"Therefore, since through God's mercy we have this ministry, we do not lose heart. Rather, we have renounced secret and shameful ways; we do not use deception, nor do we distort the word of God. On the contrary, by setting forth the truth plainly we commend ourselves to everyone's conscience in the sight of God. And even if our gospel is veiled, it is veiled to those who are perishing. The god of this age has blinded the minds of unbelievers, so that they cannot see the light of the gospel that displays the glory of Christ, who is the image of God. For what we preach is not ourselves, but Jesus Christ as Lord, and ourselves as your servants for Jesus sake. For God, who said, "Let light shine out of darkness," made his light shine in our hearts to give us the light of the knowledge of the glory of God in the face of Christ._

But we have this treasure in jars of clay to show that this all-surpassing power is from God and not from us."
— _2 Corinthians 4:1-7 (TNIV)_

This is me ...
I own nothing and no one. I am free to soar.

Journal

Chuckle Seen on the bulletin board of Jim Bob's favorite bar: "Looking for a meaningful overnight relationship."

Wisdom *"Give what you have. To someone, it may be better than you dare to think."*

— *Henry Wadsworth Longfellow*

This is me ...
I avoid looking for spectacular happiness but fully embrace contentment.

Journal

Date _____

Chuckle Jim Bob's wife Helen was chewing him out for his embarrassing behavior when she screamed: "I believe that you suffer from insanity!" Jim Bob thought calmly and then replied: "No, I actually enjoy every minute of it."

Wisdom _"Everyone who believes that Jesus is the Messiah is born of God, and everyone who loves the father loves his child as well. This is how we know that we love the children of God: by loving God and carrying out his commands. In fact, this is love for God: to obey his commands. And his commands are not burdensome, for everyone born of God overcomes the world. This is the victory that has overcome the world, even our faith. Who is it that overcomes the world? Only he who believes that Jesus is the Son of God."_

— 1 John 5:1-5 (TNIV)

This is me ...
I know that indulging in resentment is like taking a lethal dose of poison and waiting for the other person to die.

Journal

Date _____

Chuckle Did you ever stop to think and forget to start again?

Wisdom *"Every time I find myself flat on my face, I pick myself up and get back in the race.*

— *Unknown*

This is me ...
My imagination is fired by my Father God. He inspires me to conceive, undertake and complete exciting and innovative adventures that are beneficial to others, and myself as well.

Journal

Date _____

Chuckle Jim and Bob ran into each other on Monday morning.

Jim asked, "How did you spend your weekend, Bob?"

Bob answered, "Fishing through the ice."

"Fishing through the ice? For what?" asked Jim.

"Olives," replies Bob

Wisdom *"Then Jesus declared, 'I am the bread of life. Whoever comes to me will never go hungry, and whoever believes in me will never be thirsty. But as I told you, you have seen me and still you do not believe. All whom the Father gives me will come to me, and whoever comes to me I will never drive away. For I have come down from heaven not to do my will but to do the will of him who sent me. And this is the will of him who sent me; that I shall lose none of all that he has given me, but raise them up at the last day. For my Father's will is that everyone who looks to the Son and believes in him shall have eternal life, and I will raise them up at the last day.'"*
— *John 6:35-40 (TNIV)*

This is me ...
I will be raised to a new life on that day.

Journal

Date _____

Chuckle Jim Bob had his philosophy of life printed on a T-shirt: "Chaos. Panic. Disorder. My work here is done."

Wisdom _"Living itself, is a task of such immediacy, variety, beauty, and excitement that one is powerless to resist its wild embrace."_

— _E. B. White_

This is me ...
In recovery, I have discovered a short cut is one of the quickest ways to where I was not going.

Journal

Date _____

Chuckle "A committee is a group that keeps minutes and loses hours."

— _Milton Berle_

Wisdom _"The seventy-two returned with joy and said, 'Lord, even the demons submit to us in your name.' He replied, 'I saw Satan fall like lightning from heaven. I have given you authority to trample on snakes and scorpions and to overcome all the power of the enemy; nothing will harm you. However, do not rejoice that the spirits submit to you, but rejoice that your names are written in heaven.'"_

— _Luke 10:17-20 (TNIV)_

This is me ...
I am awe struck at the fact that I'm no longer in bondage to the demons that once controlled my every thought and action. Thank you, God.

Journal

Date _____

Chuckle The drunk stood confused, shivering and alone in the doorway of the AA club. His sponsor had told him that if the light was on to go in, and if the light was off to go home.

But the light was flickering.

Wisdom *"I sought my God and my God eluded me. I sought my soul and my soul eluded me. I sought my brother and I found all three."*

— William Blake

This is me ...
God is the light that never flickers in my heart.

Journal

Date _____

Chuckle Jim and Bob rented a boat and spent all day trying to catch fish. They finally found the right spot and both caught their limit.

"This is a great spot," said Jim, "We should mark it and use it again tomorrow."

"Good idea," agreed Bob, "But how can we mark it?"

"Oh that's simple," said Jim, "I'll just take my knife and cut a notch in the boat where we have both been casting."

"Man, that is the worst idea that I have ever heard," said Bob. "What if they give us a different boat tomorrow!"

Wisdom _Jesus answered, "Very truly I tell you, no one can enter the kingdom of God unless he is born of water and the Spirit. Flesh gives birth to flesh, but the Spirit gives birth to spirit. You should not be surprised at my saying, 'You must be born again.' The wind blows wherever it pleases. You hear its sound, but you cannot tell where it comes from or where it is going. So it is with everyone born of the Spirit."_

— _John 3:5-8 (TNIV)_

This is me ...
I acknowledge the reality of temptation to do wrong.
I also acknowledge the reality that God will enable me to overcome it.
I cherish those nights when I go to bed with a clear conscience.

GOD, PLEASE REWIRE MY MADFATs

JAMES BARS, BCC, CCLC
Co-author, **BLAKE BARS**

The Ultimate Treasure Chest For Love-based Living:

* God's Holy Spirit will rewire and ignite within you, inspiring, joy-filled Motives, Affections, Desires, Feelings, Actions and Thoughts—MADFATs.

* Your heart will feast on the riches of eternal wisdom, knowledge and understanding.

* You will mine the depths of advanced mind renewal emerging transformed and wealthy beyond all earthly treasure.

* You will rightly combine neuroscience, Scripture and the Holy Spirit's power with a system for success that will enrich your physical, mental, emotional and spiritual well-being.

* You will possess a clearer vision of your purpose and your soul's restoration.

* You will experience a liberating journey into the unending fortunes that are yours as a cherished member of the family of God. Yay!

Home of Love Publications

ISBN: 978-0-9817534-3-0
$17.77

available at
MyNewMADFATs.com

Exposing God Amidst The Chaos

Is God fair?
Is He loving?
Would a fair and loving God take His sick child and eternally torture that child for being born sick? This is the current view of God now portrayed to the world.
Could our perception of God be wrong?
Let's pull back the curtain and take a closer look at our God of love.

IF YOU ARE AFRAID OF GOD, SOMEONE HAS BEEN LYING TO YOU.

This is a beautiful book for souls who have been damaged by fear-based perceptions of God.

JAMES BARS, BCC, CCLC
Co-author, **BLAKE BARS**

Book Price $5.99
ISBN: 978-0-9862397-0-0

Available at
MyNewMADFATs.com

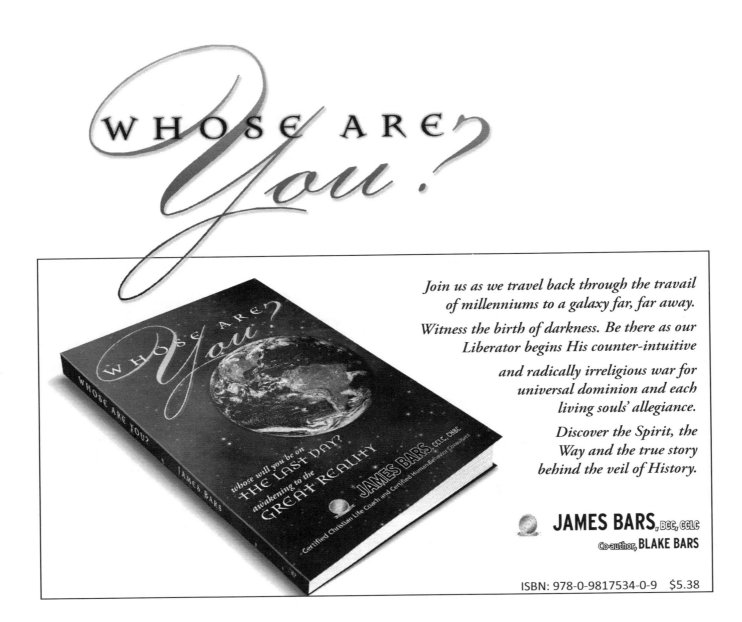

Your Own Personsal,
Christian Counselor and
Master Life Coach

James Bars – Human Behavior Consultant, Christian Counselor and Board Certified Master Life Coach

Are you... Stuck? Hurting? Broken? Burnt out? Addicted? Changing? Powerless?

In need of... Conflict Resolution! Freedom! Purpose! Balance! Direction! Fulfillment!

Explore our: *Your Inner Counselor - A Holy Spirit Guided Problem Resolution Process*

Access our: *Coaching/Counseling Services.*

We are delighted to offer clarifying, effective,

Christ-centered resources and services.

Our goal is your everlasting success!

Marriage/Relationship	Finances
Goal Setting/Accomplishment	Career/Personal Mentoring
Mid-life Crisis/Aging Concerns	Depression/Anxiety
Parenting/Blended Family Issues	Conflict/Anger Management
Addictions/Eating Disorders	Grief/Loss
Self-worth	Health/Wellness

Contact Us For Christian
Counseling & Coaching

Email: MyNewMADFATs@gmail.com
On the Web: MyNewMADFATs.com

Live Free, Love Right, Dispel the Darkness, Know the Light